THE
GHOST
AND THE
DARKNESS

ONLY THE MOST INCREDIBLE PARTS
OF THE STORY ARE TRUE

THE
GHOST
AND THE
DARKNESS

ONLY THE MOST INCREDIBLE PARTS
OF THE STORY ARE TRUE

WILLIAM GOLDMAN

CONSTELLATION FILMS PRESENTS A DOUGLAS/REUTHER PRODUCTION
A STEPHEN HOPKINS FILM MICHAEL DOUGLAS VAL KILMER
THE GHOST AND THE DARKNESS COSTUME DESIGNER ELLEN MIROJNICK LIVE EFFECTS BY STAN WINSTON
PRODUCTION DESIGNER STUART WURTZEL EDITED BY ROBERT BROWN AND STEVE MIRKOVICH, A.C.E.
DIRECTOR OF PHOTOGRAPHY VILMOS ZSIGMOND, A.S.C. CO-PRODUCER GRANT HILL
EXECUTIVE PRODUCERS MICHAEL DOUGLAS AND STEVEN REUTHER WRITTEN BY WILLIAM GOLDMAN
PRODUCED BY GALE ANNE HURD, PAUL RADIN AND A. KITMAN HO
DIRECTED BY STEPHEN HOPKINS

DISTRIBUTED BY PARAMOUNT PICTURES CORPORATION
TM & COPYRIGHT © 1996 BY PARAMOUNT PICTURES ALL RIGHTS RESERVED

APPLAUSE
NEW YORK • LONDON

An Applause Original

THE GHOST AND THE DARKNESS by William Goldman

Copyright © 1996 by Mont Blanc Entertainment GmbH

Library of Congress Cataloging-in-Publication Data

LC Catalog # 96-078576

British Library Cataloging-in-Publication Data

A catalogue record for this book is available from the British Library

ISBN: 1-55783-267-6

APPLAUSE BOOKS
211 West 71st Street
New York, NY 10023
Phone: (212) 496-7511
Fax: (212) 721-2856

A&C Black
Howard Road
Huntington, Cambs PE19 3EZ
Phone: 0171-242 0946
Fax: 0171-831-8478

INTRODUCTION

To put far too fine a point on it, this is the start of my fifth decade of professional writing. (I began my first novel, *The Temple of Gold*, on June 25, 1956, and it is now forty years and one month later.) And in that time, I have come across but two great true pieces of material. The first, dealing with Butch Cassidy and his adventures with the Sundance Kid became a famous movie around the world. But it was unknown material before that.

The second is the tale of the man eating lion of Tsavo, which is well known around the world, just not in the United States today. In Africa, it is the most famous story of high adventure. A hunt for wild animals is called a "stalk" and no less an aficionado than President Theodore Roosevelt termed it "the greatest stalk of which we have any record." More recently, in his splendid book *Millennium, A History of the Last Thousand Years*, the Oxford historian Felipe Fernandez-Armesto has written over seven hundred pages on what's been going on Down Here for the last ten centuries.

Well, two of those pages are about the lions of Tsavo.

Why were Butch and Sundance unknown for so long? I think because they ran away to South America when the Superposse came after them, instead of shooting it out, which is what Western heroes always did, since Westerns are based on confrontations

I think the reason the Tsavo lions are unknown here is because, when Americans go to the movies we want solutions to questions, not more questions. (As I write this, national frustration over the explosion TWA 800 keeps growing — we all want it to have been an explosion. Set by Bad Guys. Then we can nuke 'em. And get back to the really important stuff, Matthew and Gwyneth.) The Tsavo story, something that never happened before and has not happened since, is still, at its dark heart, a mystery.

And always will be.

I first heard about them in July of 1984, my initial trip to Africa, on the Masai Mara plains. It was night, a bunch of people were sitting by a fire. And then, in that magical semi-darkness someone began telling the story of what happened in Tsavo back in 1898. And I clearly remember that I turned to Ilene, my good wife of twenty some years, and said something I had never said before: "that's a movie."

My plan then was simple — to research the story back in America, to return to Africa in two years for further work, and then to write it as an original screenplay. Life, however, as most of us are continually shocked to discover, has plans of its own which tend to take precedence. I did a lot of research when I returned home, yes. But our marriage ended, the further trips to Africa never took place, and the lions found a small corner of my brain, growled, and went to sleep.

Dissolve, as they say Out There, for five years. It's 1989.

I got a call from my agent, Robert Bookman of CAA. "You remember the lion story?" I said I sure did. "Well, there's some interest in the project at Paramount. Do you have a problem flying to L.A. to try for the job?"

I said I had zero problem flying to L.A.

But there was indeed a problem.

My back.

It was out.

I have a bad back and it tends to go into spasm when it chooses — crippling me, usually for a week or two. And it had gone out just before Bookman called. And when that happens the worst thing is having to sit in a car for a long time. Having to sit in an airplane for a long time also isn't so terrific. I made the trip the next day, met with the Paramount guys. The usual bullshit grunts of hello. Then it was my turn to sell.

This is not something for which I am noted. I have only tried one "pitch" in my life, and that was for friends, and I was so awful I quit half way through. And now I was sitting in a room with a bunch of strangers. More precisely, *they* were sitting in the room.

Me, I was lying on the floor.

Pretty much in a spasm.

Looking up at them.

I said I had no idea how to write the movie. I said I had no idea yet what the story was. But I also said I knew what the story *should* be: a cross between *Jaws* and *Lawrence of Arabia*. I said that they could doubt my talent to be able to successfully write that movie, but they could never doubt my passion for wanting to try — I mean shit, I was flying six thousand miles more or less doubled over, that had to be indicative of something. (I was told the meeting, because of my position, achieved a certain brief notoriety.)

At any rate, I was hired.

I delivered the first draft on April Fool's Day, 1990. I always aim for that date — after all, we *are* talking about the movie business. Shortly afterwards, we met again, the Paramount Guys (PG's) and *moi*. Here is what they said: yes, we like the script, yes, we think it's a movie. But it is also going to be a very very expensive movie. So we will only make it if we can get one of these three stars to play Patterson, the main character:

Costner

Cruise

Gibson.

Well, those happen to be wonderful performers, and all three were good casting for the role. Serious about their careers and their choices of material. And huge stars.

The problem is, you just don't get people like that for pictures like this. (Neither O'Toole nor Scheider nor Dreyfus nor Shaw were huge stars.) Because stars know they are inevitably going to be dwarfed by the desert of the monster. And in the case of *The Ghost and the Darkness*, I knew none of Paramount's holy trinity would sit around while lions ate the movie. So while I said "terrific" to the studio about their casting choices, I've been at this awhile and I have a certain sense for failure when it is coming hard upon. I knew, in other words, none of the three would do it. The movie was dead in the water.

A week later, Kevin Costner said 'yes.'

One of the points to keep in mind when talking about movie stars is this: not only do we change, *they* change. So today when people disparage the lovely Miss Roberts and wonder why she isn't that smiling star of *Pretty Woman*, the answer is pretty easy: that child is gone. Roberts was 22 then, and we knew nothing much about her, and we all fell in love. Well, she's closing in on thirty now, we know *everything* about her, some of it a bit disquieting, and our ardor has cooled. If she did a sequel to *Pretty Woman* now, and she might if her career gets rocky enough, I would love to be a fly on the wall when the poor screenwriter has to come up with a plausible scene explaining where Julia has been hooking all these years.

The Kevin Costner of today, we know about: the divorce, the *Waterworld* budget, all that good stuff. But we're still in 1990, remember, and *Dances With Wolves* is about to explode across the world, catapulting Costner into an atmosphere few stars ever attain. Remember how we rooted for him, putting his career on the line to do an ugh, Western? A three hour ugh Western at that. And not just to star, but for the first time to direct?

Well, he gambled and won and we didn't just love him, we carried him through our village shoulder high. And as I flew out to the next meeting with the PG's, I knew that after a half a dozen years, the Gods were smiling.

"We know what we said last week," the PG's began. "We know we said we would only do it with Costner or Gibson or Cruise. And we are thrilled that Kevin wants to do it so badly. That only proves what we felt about the value of the material. And since Costner agreed so quickly, we now know what we have to do."

And then a pause.

Not just any pause. This baby poised hovering on the horizon was one of the longer lulls of my young life.

Because then, oh then, he spoke the most dreaded of all phrases: "*special relationship.*"

There is something you must understand about studio executives — (and these guys were absolutely standard; bright, decent, hard working — though they were shortly to be fired for helping run the company right off a cliff). Studio executives *love* stars. Because these are the executives' two eternal verities —

1) — they are all going to get fired —

but 2) — if they can just sign enough stars to enough flicks, they will delay their beheading.

Perfectly understandable behavior. When it gets dangerous is this: it is not enough to love stars; in their continually fevered brains they want to believe that *stars also love them*. And so over the decades I have heard that "Sly and I have a special relationship" and "Dusty and I have a special relationship" and Arnold and I and Clint and I and Marlon and I and Paul and I and Steve and I and backward reeleth the mind.

The truth is this: stars do not now give and never have given even half a shit for studio executives. Stars only care, absolutely legitimately and correctly, about two things, the material and the money.

But studio executives, poor, put upon, terrified, underappreciated, like the rest of us, dream of being loved.

"We have a special relationship with Tom Cruise," the head PG said that day. "We are doing a picture with Tom now and we want this to be his next. He has a lot on his plate at the moment, yes, but we are prepared to wait for him. Because we know he'll love this. And we know he loves working with us."

We waited six months for an answer. The movie he was starting was indeed a plateful. It was called *Days of Thunder* and it was not the easiest shoot ever undertaken and not only that, he was also producing.

He passed.

Costner had taken off five months and three weeks before, very pissed off and with very good reason. We never went to Gibson. No point. There was now no movie. And honestly, I felt there never would be.

The Tsavo lions curled up inside my brain again and slept for five more years . . .

Which is not to say there was zero action. Michael Douglas, who has a remarkable record as a producer (he won the Oscar for his first try, *One Flew Over the Cuckoo's Nest*) and his partner Stephen Reuther came aboard. And Stephen Hopkins was selected to direct. Stirrings, sure. But lots of movies get producers, bring directors on, then disappear. We needed what used to be called Out There a "locomotive."

In other words, a male star. Optimist that I have always been, I knew we would never get one.

But as the sadly missed Mr. Williams once wrote for Miss DuBois, "Sometimes there's God so quickly." Because our Salvation was taking place across town, on the Warner Brothers lot, where a wonderful actor, Michael Keaton, had what I can only call the most helpful fit of madness of my career.

Understand this about stars: *they do not want to appear in commercial films.* Oh, some will put up with them. Harrison Ford owes his entire career to three series, Star Wars and Indiana Jones and Tom Clancy. Stallone exists today because of Rocky and Rambo. Mel Gibson also had two, Mad Max and the Lethal Weapons. But these are not the norm.

And Michael Keaton chose to ignore the ecology of Hollywood — you do one for me, I'll do one for you. He had been in the first *Batman*, which Jack Nicholson stole. He had done the second, this time bowing to Pfeiffer and DeVito. And that, apparently, was enough. He did not want to don the dreaded Bat suit again. He felt the part wasn't terrific. And you know what? Dead right. Batman was this stiff the others got to be flashy by playing off of.

So he walked.

And Val Kilmer replaced him.

Val Kilmer who, it turned out, *loved* Africa.

Once more the phone rang from Hollywood. The lions answered it with me. We were alive again. Because the new Paramount people had always liked the Tsavo script. And suddenly there was this hot new star who wanted to play Patterson. *Batman Forever* had not opened yet. But the advance word was sensational.

Suddenly we were a "go."

And that's how movies get made.

A dozen years have passed since the first night on the Masai Mara. We might have come out in '91, in place of *Robin Hood*. We might not have come out in '96, because if Keaton stuck with Batman, no way a studio would have sent us into production.

Wouldda, shouldda, couldda, here we are.

—William Goldman

THE
GHOST
AND THE
DARKNESS

FADE IN ON

A TINY FIGURE OF A MAN *hurrying toward camera. The figure gets larger as he approaches. But as yet we cannot tell who he is or where we are.*

> MALE VOICE (over)
> This is the most famous true story of Africa. It happened a hundred years ago, but even now, when children ask about it, you do not tell them at night.
> *(THE FIGURE continues to grow)*
> It began with the race to build a railroad across Africa.
> *(beat)*
> But this is not about building a railroad—it is about Patterson.

And now we can tell that the FIGURE *is a* YOUNG MAN, *a* LIEUTENANT COLONEL. *This is* PATTERSON. *He is gifted and bright and serious, serious about his life, serious about his career. He has been successful in everything he's attempted, in part because of his talents, in part because he is willing to outwork anybody.*

AND THIS IS WHERE WE ARE: ENGLAND.

More specifically, in a high-ceilinged corridor of an elegant building—lovely woodwork all around. Everything is neat, everything is clean and in order.

> MALE VOICE (over)
> Patterson was thirty. A brilliant engineer. A fine man, but do not become attached to him— there are many fine men in this story but do not become attached to any of them.
> *(beat)*
> So many of them die.

PATTERSON *stops at a large ornate door, knocks. Waits.*

> MALE VOICE (over)
> And remember this: only the impossible parts of what follow really happened . . .
> *(Now the door opens and we—)*

CUT TO

Just a wonderfully handsome man standing in the doorway. This is ROBERT BEAUMONT—*40, with an irresistible smile. We're in his office and the place reflects the man—clean, cold. There are maps and charts on the walls. He ushers* PATTERSON *inside.*

> **BEAUMONT**
> *(The great smile flashes)*
> John Henry Patterson, come in, I'm Robert Beaumont.
> *(They shake hands)*
> Firm—I like that, tells me a lot about you—
> *(beat)*
> —now why don't you tell me about me? To get you started, many peo-
> ple find me handsome, with a wonderful smile. I'm sure you agree.
> *(Surprised, uncomfortable,*
> *PATTERSON nods)*
> Winning personality, heaps of charm?

> **PATTERSON**
> My wife is the game player in the family, sir.

> **BEAUMONT**
> Games?
> *(staring dead at PATTERSON)*
> Look at me closely, Patterson: I am a *monster*. My only pleasure is
> tormenting people who work for me, such as yourself.
> *(again the smile—only now it's chilling)*
> One mistake and I promise you this: I'll make you hate me.

CUT TO

PATTERSON, *as he realizes* BEAUMONT *is serious.* BEAUMONT *turns sharply and moves to a large map.*

CUT TO

THE MAP. *It covers a great deal of East Africa with a very clear line that ends at Lake Victoria, a distance of some 600 miles.*

> **BEAUMONT**
> *(pointing along the line)*
> We are building this railroad across Africa for the glorious purpose
> of saving Africa from the Africans. And, of course, to end slavery.
> The Germans and French are our competition. We are ahead, and
> we will stay ahead providing you do what I hired you to do—

CUT TO

A MORE DETAILED MAP. *This one ends at "Tsavo," 130 miles in.*

BEAUMONT

—build the bridge over the Tsavo river. And be finished in four months time. Can you do that?

PATTERSON

I'm sure you've examined my record. So you know I've never yet been late on a bridge.

BEAUMONT

You've never built in Africa.

PATTERSON

But I have in India—every country presents problems.

BEAUMONT

You'll need your confidence, I promise you.

PATTERSON

I've got a reason far beyond confidence: my wife is having our firstborn in five months and I promised I'd be with her when the baby comes.

BEAUMONT

Very moving, Patterson; I'm touched you confided in me.
                    (beat)
But I don't really give a shit about your upcoming litter. I've made you with this assignment—
                    (the smile)
—don't make me break you.

PATTERSON
                    (smiling right back)
You won't have the chance.
                    (glancing at his watch)
Any further words of encouragement?
                    (silence)
Then I've a train to catch.

They look at each other a moment in silence—and it's very clear they do not like each other. PATTERSON turns, leaves and we

CUT TO

A RAILWAY STATION, IMMEDIATELY AFTER.

A train is loading up. A lot of activity, a lot of noise. PATTERSON stands in the midst of it, anxiously looking around.

CUT TO

HELENA PATTERSON, hurrying through the crowd. Early 20s, with the kind of serene beauty of Jean Simmons. She is still slim, has not begun to show. She spots him, puts a smile on, goes straight into his arms.

> **HELENA**
>
> I tried to be late, John—it would have been easier if you'd gone.

> **PATTERSON**
> *(They are nutty about
> each other—he nods)*
>
> We're not much good at goodbyes, Helena.

> **HELENA**
> *(brightly)*
>
> Tell me about Beaumont—does he understand how brilliant you are, how lucky he is to have you?

> **PATTERSON**
> *(nods)*
>
> It was embarrassing—the man showered me with compliments.

They start to walk hand in hand along the platform toward a quieter place. PATTERSON is suddenly very serious—

> **HELENA**
>
> Oh dear—
> *(beat)*
> —you're getting that downtrodden look again—

> **PATTERSON**
>
> —well, it's just . . .
> *(beat)*
> . . . other men don't abandon their wives at such a time—

> **HELENA**
> *(not unkindly)*
>
> —oh please—if I'd been against your taking this, you *would* have abandoned me. You've been desperate to see Africa your whole life.

> **PATTERSON**
>
> What if there are complications?—

> **HELENA**
>
> —not "what if"—there *will* be, there always are. Which only means that our "son" and I—note my confidence—will have an excuse to come visit.

THE TRAIN WHISTLE sounds.

> **HELENA**
>
> Go, now.
>
>   *(He kisses her hand)*
>
> Such a gentleman.
>
>   *(Now he holds her)*

> **PATTERSON**
>
> I am desperate to see Africa—but I hate the leaving.

CUT TO

HELENA. She hates it, too.

> **HELENA**
>
> You build bridges, John—
>
>   *(beat)*
>
> —you've got to go where the rivers are.

They hold each other a moment more, then break, then back into each other's arms a final time, then—

CUT TO

THE TRAIN, and thick clouds of steam—

—PATTERSON runs into the clouds and disappears.

HOLD FOR A MOMENT.

KEEP HOLDING.

PATTERSON runs out of the steam and we

PULL BACK TO REVEAL

A DIFFERENT TRAIN, A DIFFERENT COUNTRY, A DIFFERENT WORLD.

This is the train to TSAVO and PATTERSON is alone on the engine seat—a wooden *bench in <u>front</u> of the engine used by railroad inspectors and visiting VIPs. Behind it is a white circular piece of wood used to keep the engine heat from the passengers.*

CUT TO

NIGEL STARLING, running as best he can alongside the train, trying to pull himself up onto the engine seat.

STARLING is a terribly appealing young man. Clothes do not fit him well, and he is constantly tugging at this sleeve or that shirttail, trying to get things right. He wears glasses, tends nonetheless to squint at the world. He is, above all, a good man, morally impeccable and very much a product of these Victorian times.

> **STARLING**
> *(as PATTERSON helps him aboard)*
>
> Many thanks.
> *(squints)*
> You're Patterson, yes?
> *(PATTERSON nods)*
> Nigel Starling—I'll be assisting you at Tsavo—but surely Beaumont must have told you that.

> **PATTERSON**
>
> He just gave me his "monster" speech.

> **STARLING**
>
> That. I know Robert seems dreadful, but when you truly get to know the man, well, he's much worse.
> *(beat)*
> And I'm one of his defenders.
> *(PATTERSON smiles)*
> Forget him for now—it's your first ride to Tsavo—I think you'll find it breathtaking.
> *(And on that word—)*

CUT TO

STARLING coughing like crazy, hands over his face which is caked with dust—he and PATTERSON stare out at an absolutely dreary desert.

> **PATTERSON**
> *(shouting toward STARLING)*
>
> "Breathtaking" doesn't begin to do it justice.
> *(As STARLING starts to laugh, his*

mouth opens and sand flies in, and
his coughing fit returns and)

CUT TO

THE DESERT. ENDLESS. LATER IN THE DAY.

CUT TO

THE TWO OF THEM, bent over, arms covering their faces as the dust gets worse—a
wind has kicked up.

CUT TO

**THE TRAIN, TRYING TO MAKE IT UP A STEEP GRADE. STILL
LATER.**

PATTERSON and STARLING are walking beside the train now, helping to push it,
trudging through the dust. All the other passengers spread out behind them, also
pushing—the train obviously needs all the assistance it can get.

CUT TO

INSIDE A RAILROAD CAR, EARLY EVENING.

PATTERSON and STARLING, filthy, sit together. STARLING has nodded off. PATTER-
SON has a book open in his lap—

—we can tell there are drawings of African animals—not all that accurate.

Now PATTERSON's eyes close and he sleeps.

CUT TO

THE TRAIN POUNDING THROUGH THE NIGHT.

Stokers shovel coal. They are exhausted but they keep at it.

CUT TO

**PATTERSON. WAKING IN THE CAR, RUBBING HIS EYES. IT'S
DAWN.**

He stares out—

—and from his face it's clear something special has happened. And now, at last—

CUT TO

SOMETHING SPECIAL—*and what it is, of course, is* PATTERSON's *first view of the Africa of his imagination.*

Because the desert has ended, and now there are grasses and trees and one more thing—

—bursts of animals. On both sides of the train.

A flock of birds materializes here, a cluster of gazelles doing their amazing leap there.

PATTERSON *is like a kid in a candy store.*

CUT TO

PATTERSON *and* STARLING, *back outside in the engine seat again.* STARLING *points—*

> **STARLING**
> Aren't they amazing?

CUT TO

WHAT HE'S POINTING AT: *Some giraffes running along, their absurd shape suddenly graceful as they eat up the ground in incredibly long strides.*

CUT TO

PATTERSON *and* STARLING, *staring out.*

> **PATTERSON**
> You know the most amazing thing about them? —they only sleep
> five minutes a day.
> *(STARLING glances at him—
> clearly, he didn't know that)*

CUT TO

A FAMILY OF HYENAS. *Close by, loping in their scary way.*

> **STARLING**
> Don't much like them.

> **PATTERSON**
> *(nods)*
> The females are bigger—only animal here like that—have to be or
> they wouldn't survive because the males eat the young.

CUT TO

STARLING *studying* PATTERSON. *Clearly, he didn't know that, either.*

CUT TO

SOME HIPPOS moving along. STARLING turns to PATTERSON.

> **STARLING**
> Anything special about them?

> **PATTERSON**
> Just that they fart through their mouths.
> *(beat)*
> Must make kissing something of a gamble.

> **STARLING**
> *(laughs)*
> I've lived in Africa a year and I don't know what you know. How long have you been here?

> **PATTERSON**
> *(looks at his watch)*
> Almost three hours.
> *(beat)*
> But I've been getting ready all my life.
> *(Now, from them—)*

CUT TO

A BUNCH OF IMPOVERISHED-LOOKING NATIVE WOMEN. They hold children who wave at the passing train. The children are more impoverished looking than their mothers.

> **STARLING**
> *(suddenly touched)*
> Every time I see something like that, I know we're right to be here— to bring Christianity into their lives, enrich their souls.

> **PATTERSON**
> Beaumont says it's to end slavery.

> **STARLING**
> *(shrugs)*
> We all have our reasons. Mine is simply to make them understand happiness, accept salvation, know the serenity that comes—
> *(interrupts himself)*
> —best I stop. One of the by-products of my belief is that I can become amazingly boring. But I know God smiles on me.

> PATTERSON
> *(They really like each other)*
> Have you got that in writing?
> *(STARLING, amazingly good natured,*
> *laughs. And now)*

CUT TO

A WHITE CLAW.

PULL BACK TO REVEAL

Hundreds of white claws.

KEEP PULLING BACK TO REVEAL

They aren't claws at all, they're thorns as sharp as claws and they're on a twenty foot high thorn tree.

And there are dozens of those trees, packed together. All mixed in with other trees, low and stunted, and thick underbrush and baked red rocks—

—now the train begins to slow.

Smoke drifts across.

A bunch of wildebeest scatter off the tracks.

> STARLING *(over)*
> Welcome to Tsavo.
> *(on the word)*

CUT TO

TSAVO.

We have arrived at the train station area and what we see is a place that is still being built. There are tin shacks; a water tower is under construction, tents are under construction—

—men are working everywhere, for that's what Tsavo is: a place for work.

THE TRAIN goes slower still.

No one stands idly around here.

But no one looks happy either.

ONE MAN is apart from the rest: this is SAMUEL.

An ageless Masai, tall and slender, he has a smile that can light the world.

CUT TO

PATTERSON and STARLING as they step off the train.

> **STARLING**
> *(indicating SAMUEL,*
> *who is approaching)*

Samuel is camp liaison—absolutely indispensable—the only man here everyone trusts.

> **PATTERSON**
> *(softly)*

Does he speak English?

> **SAMUEL**
> *(not softly enough)*

And very poor French.

> **STARLING**
> *(introducing)*

Samuel—John Patterson.

> **SAMUEL**
> *(as they shake)*

The bridgebuilder—
> *(gesturing to the working men)*
—we have been getting ready for you.

> **PATTERSON**

Excellent. Could I see the bridge site?
> *(SAMUEL nods)*

> **STARLING**

I've got medical supplies to deliver. Come along to the hospital when you're done.
> *(starting off)*

> **SAMUEL**

I will bring him, Nigel.

We should realize by now that SAMUEL's was the voice we heard at the very beginning of the picture.

CUT TO

PATTERSON *and* SAMUEL, *starting to walk. They pass the water tower.*

Standing on top of it in a precarious position is an extremely powerful INDIAN. *He waves to* SAMUEL *who waves back. This is* SINGH.

WORKERS *study* PATTERSON *as he moves by. Not smiling. Up ahead, some* SIKHS *are erecting tents. Not smiling.*

> **PATTERSON**
> Why do the workers look unhappy?

> **SAMUEL**
> Because they are here.
> *(beat)*
> Because Tsavo is the worst place in the world.
> *(He points ahead)*
> Come, John—to the bridge.
> *(And on that—)*

CUT TO

THE RAILROAD TRACKS *as the camera pans along.*

CUT TO

THE RIVER *in the distance as they walk toward it.*

And here is as good a place as any to explain just what the spot where the movie takes place was like.

There were five hundred men working for PATTERSON. *And they lived in a spread out area. A bunch of Indian coolies who might have come from the same town back in their country might choose to live in one cluster of tents. A group of natives might be in another cluster.*

What we have then, as far as living places are concerned, are dozens of clusters of tents. (Eventually, as the terror began, these areas all got surrounded, each with its own thorn fence.)

The places we'll come to know best are, among others, PATTERSON's *living area, the hospital tent area, the area by the river where the bridge is to be built, etc., etc.*

As they move, SAMUEL *points out various camps.*

A SECT OF INDIANS *is getting ready for prayer.*

ANOTHER SECT OF INDIANS is eating.

A GROUP OF AFRICANS are cleaning their tent area.

Anyway, you get the idea. Just remember that the place covered a wide expanse, maybe a mile square, maybe more.

Okay, back to the story.

> **PATTERSON**
> *(as they pass the INDIAN tent area*
> *where prayer is starting)*
> It's all wonderfully under control, Samuel—you've done a splendid job.

> **SAMUEL**
> Thank you. The truth is this: you have to work at it constantly.

> **PATTERSON**
> The workers don't get on?

> **SAMUEL**
> Get on? They detest each other. Obviously the Africans hate the Indians. But the Indians also hate the other Indians. Some of them worship cows, while others eat them.
> *(As they move on)*

CUT TO

RAILROAD TRACK.

PAN ALONG TO

MORE RAILROAD TRACK.

KEEP PANNING

And suddenly the track just stops in mid-air as we

PULL BACK TO REVEAL

PATTERSON and SAMUEL standing high above the Tsavo River. The track has come to the edge of the area above the riverbank—where it just stops—

—and picks up on the far side. All that's missing, in other words, is the hundred-yard-long bridge that will connect the pieces of track.

> SAMUEL
> *(to the far side)*

Railhead is across there.

CUT TO

THE DISTANCE. *Nothing can be made out clearly but there are great clouds of dust.*

> SAMUEL

Three thousand men laying track—when the bridge is done, it all joins up.

PATTERSON nods, says nothing, but goes to his haunches, staring at the space where the bridge is to be.

> SAMUEL

Did it look like this in your mind?

> PATTERSON
> *(shakes his head)*

This is more difficult—

CUT TO

PATTERSON. CLOSE UP. *Excited.*

> PATTERSON
> *(eyes bright)*

—but how wonderful that it's difficult, it should be difficult—what better job in all the world than build a bridge? —make things connect—bring worlds together—and get it right!
> *(Now from PATTERSON—)*

CUT TO

THE HOSPITAL TENT

as PATTERSON and SAMUEL walk in. PATTERSON glances around—

—it's not bad at all. Of course there are some patients, injured or with fever. But like the rest of the camp we've just seen, everything is working well, everything is under control. STARLING approaches.

> STARLING

Finish your tour?

> **PATTERSON**
> *(nods)*

And anxious to get started.
> *(indicating the hospital)*

What is this, mostly malaria?

> **STARLING**

Yes—but their suffering is only transitory—once they accept God into their hearts, He will vanquish all pain.

> **MAN'S VOICE** (over)

That's just vomitous talk, Nigel—the poor bastards will relapse if you keep on that way.
> *(As they turn—)*

CUT TO

DOCTOR DAVID HAWTHORNE. *A tough, middle-aged cockney. And a heavy drinker. A man who hasn't been tactful in twenty years.*

> **HAWTHORNE**
> *(to PATTERSON)*

I'm David Hawthorne, this is my hospital. And my advice to you is, "don't get sick in front of it."
> *(beat)*

That was meant to be charming, sorry. I seem to have lost the knack.

> **STARLING**

You never had it.

> **HAWTHORNE**

Nigel and I don't like each other much.

> **SAMUEL**
> *(breaking the tension)*

I am also liaison between these two.

> **PATTERSON**
> *(to HAWTHORNE)*

Clearly you don't agree about building the railroad?

> **HAWTHORNE**

This sham? Ridiculous. Who needs it? It's only being built to control the ivory trade, make rich men richer.

> PATTERSON

Then why do you stay?

> HAWTHORNE

Who else would hire me?
> *(to STARLING)*

Beat you to it, didn't I?
> *(beat)*

Oh yes, almost forgot—brought you a little welcoming gift.
> *(Now he gestures and we—)*

CUT TO

A NERVOUS ORDERLY who approaches them. He has been freshly bandaged across one shoulder.

> HAWTHORNE

This is Karim, one of my orderlies—attacked by a man-eater earlier today—first incident of that kind here.

PATTERSON says not a word, just studies the wounded man.

> STARLING
> *(incredulous)*

A man-eater attacks and you're such a buffoon you almost forget to mention it?

> HAWTHORNE

Well, he got away, didn't he?
> *(to PATTERSON)*

Riding a donkey not far from here when the lion sprang on them— donkey took the brunt of it—then suddenly the lion ran off.

CUT TO

PATTERSON. Listening. No emotion on his face.

CUT TO

HAWTHORNE. He's kind of enjoying this. Bearing down.

> HAWTHORNE

I know it's your first day and of course you must be tired from the journey—
> *(beat)*

—but what are you going to do about it?

PATTERSON
(a long pause, then evenly—)
Karim will have to show me where it happened. And of course, I'll need the donkey.
(beat)
With any luck, I'll sort it out tonight.
(And he walks out, leaving an aston-ished STARLING staring after him.

CUT TO

PATTERSON'S TENT AREA.

STARLING has a tent there, too, as do SAMUEL and HAWTHORNE. And there are half a dozen ORDERLIES.

Right now, PATTERSON is unpacking, moving in and out of his tent. STARLING, sipping tea, sits and watches.

STARLING
I couldn't believe it when you said "sort it out." As if it were the most normal thing in the world. "Ho-hum, what lovely tea, I think I'll bag a killer beast this evening, nothing much else going on anyway."

PATTERSON
Well, he put me in a spot, didn't he? But that's all right—after all, I'm responsible for everything that happens here. And it certainly won't do much for morale if a man-eater's on the prowl.

He goes into his tent with some books now and we go with him. There is a photo of HELENA on a small table. A photo of AN ELDERLY COUPLE, clearly his parents. His clothes are stacked with precision. He arranges his books precisely too.

Clearly, JOHN PATTERSON is a man who believes in order.

STARLING
(calling out)
You said "of course" you'd need the donkey. Why "of course"?

PATTERSON
(taking a rifle, moving outside)
We know three things about man-eaters. First, they *always* return to where they've attacked before. Second, they're *always* old—they can't catch other animals so they turn to us. And third, they're *always* alone—they've been cast out by their pride because they can't keep up.

CUT TO

STARLING, *sipping his tea and there's no hiding it, he's excited. But also a bit reluctant.*

> **STARLING**
> I don't suppose I could watch.

> **PATTERSON**
> *(delighted)*
> Might be exciting for you.

> **STARLING**
> I've never been all that adventurous. I wouldn't be in the way?

> **PATTERSON**
> I'd love the company. And I've hunted all my life.

> **STARLING**
> *(gathering courage)*
> Well, why not? You seem so calm and experienced.
> *(standing, teacup in hand)*
> Why not, indeed!
> *(Now from that—)*

CUT TO

A SLIGHTLY WOUNDED DONKEY.

It's roped loosely to a tree, bells around its neck. When it moves, they make a sound. Middle of the night. A night wind.

PULL BACK TO REVEAL

We're in a clearing with thick trees all around.

KEEP PULLING BACK TO REVEAL

PATTERSON *and* STARLING, *seated uncomfortably in a tree on the edge of the clearing, twelve feet up in the air.* PATTERSON *has his rifle ready. This next is all whispered.*

> **STARLING**
> *(embarrassed)*
> I hate to be a bother, John, but the cramp's getting worse.
> *(Pulls up his trousers—*
> *his leg is knotted)*
> The pain is actually quite unbearable now.

> PATTERSON

Shhh.

> STARLING

I'm sure you mean that to be comforting, but—

> PATTERSON
> *(interrupting)*
> —you'll have to deal with it, Nigel.

> STARLING

That is precisely my plan—but back in my tent.
> *(And he begins to climb down)*

CUT TO

PATTERSON, *grabbing him.*

> PATTERSON

They own the night—nobody moves when there's a man-eater out there.

STARLING *glumly obeys. Then—*

> STARLING

John? I know this isn't the time to ask, but—

> PATTERSON

What?

> STARLING

Since you'd only been here three hours when we met, are you sure this is how you hunt lions?

> PATTERSON

Not to terrify you, Nigel, but it's worse than you think—I've never even *seen* one.

CUT TO

STARLING, *not pleased with this news. He massages his calf, tries to get comfortable, which is impossible.* PATTERSON *just stares at the night.*

CUT TO

JUST BEFORE DAWN.

The donkey dozes. So does STARLING. PATTERSON *has not so much as moved.*

Now the bushes behind the donkey shake just a little.

And the donkey is suddenly awake and scared—

—and then it all goes crazy—the donkey screams and a lion appears from the bushes and PATTERSON *fires one shot and the sound* **explodes—**

—and STARLING *topples from the tree to the ground, landing shocked but unhurt—*

—he has landed close to the dead lion—he stares at it.

>   STARLING
>   *(amazed)*
> . . . one shot . . .

>   PATTERSON
>   *(even more amazed)*
> So that's what a lion looks like.
>   *(Now from the tree—)*

CUT TO

THE HOSPITAL TENT AREA. JUST AFTER DAWN.

HOLD for a moment.

>   SAMUEL *(over)*
> One shot—*one—*

KEEP HOLDING.

Now SAMUEL *comes walking into the shot, really excited—*

—it's the first time we've seen his wonderful smile.

>   SAMUEL
> Patterson has made the nights safe again.

KEEP HOLDING FOR JUST A MOMENT MORE.

As he walks on, behind him come THREE COOLIES *carrying the body of the lion. As dozens of men come running in from all over to see the dead man-eater—*

>   SAMUEL
>   *(mimes shooting)*
> BOOM!
>   *(Now as the crowd continues to grow—)*

CUT TO

A ROUGH ENGINEER'S DRAWING OF WHAT WILL BE THE BRIDGE.

It has two embankments on either side of the river.

These embankments are <u>big</u>—forty feet wide, fifty feet high.

CUT TO

PATTERSON and STARLING standing on the high ground where the embankment will start. From here, there is a slope down to the river itself.

Also present is UNGAN SINGH, who we saw earlier standing precariously atop the water tower. SINGH, enormously powerful, is another assistant. Bright, a great worker, another main character in what is to follow.

Now PATTERSON starts to walk down the slope towards the river—it's not that easy to do without falling, but that doesn't bother him. He talks and gestures as he explains to the other two who move down with him.

SINGH, for all his massive size, moves like a cat. STARLING does not, slipping and sliding.

> **PATTERSON**
> *(gesturing)*
> All right, I'd like to start the embankments today—
> *(to SINGH)*
> —sufficient supplies on hand?

> **SINGH**
> *(nods)*
> More than.

> **STARLING**
> With much more on the way—
> *(loses balance, falls)*
> —John—we could have had this chat on flatter ground—

> **PATTERSON**
> —true enough—but without the comedy relief.
> *(STARLING, amazingly good natured,
> smiles, gets back up.)*

CUT TO

THE RIVER as they scramble down to it.

CUT TO

THE SLOPE they've come down—it's a long way back to the top.

CUT TO

THE THREE MEN. It's a glorious morning.

> PATTERSON
>
> How lucky we are.

> STARLING
>
> Aren't we full of ourselves today?
> *(beat)*
> I think it's because of the lion.

> PATTERSON
>
> Possibly.

> SINGH
> *(soft)*
> You know, I too have killed a lion.

> STARLING
>
> How many shots did you need?

CUT TO

SINGH. Almost embarrassed.

> SINGH
>
> I used my hands.

He holds his big hands up, palms out. STARLING looks at SINGH to see if he means it—

—he means it all right. Now, from STARLING's perpetually surprised face—

CUT TO

SURVEYING EQUIPMENT.

PULL BACK TO REVEAL

PATTERSON sighting through it—we are on the far side of the river now. SINGH is there, STARLING, too.

Behind them: a field of tall grass.

> **PATTERSON**
>
> All right—the second embankment will go there.
> > *(He gestures toward the river)*

> **STARLING**
>
> You do plan to mark it a bit more precisely than just—
> > *(imitating PATTERSON)*
>
> —"there."

> **PATTERSON**
> > *(smiles)*
>
> In your honor, Nigel. And you and Singh will be in charge of building them—and you'll also build the roadbeds and the three foundation pillars—and you'll be finished in eight thrilling weeks.

> **STARLING**
> > *(very dubious)*
>
> John, it will not be easy.

> **PATTERSON**
>
> Nigel, you'll just have to use your hands—
> > *(And he smiles, repeating SINGH's*
> > *gesture, both palms out)*

CUT TO

SINGH. *He smiles back, starts to reply. But his words stop, his smile dies. He just stares and we—*

CUT TO

WHAT HE'S STARING AT—*the surrounding field of tall grass. Nothing unusual about it.*

CUT TO

PATTERSON. *He stares, too.*

CUT TO

THE FIELD OF TALL GRASS—*suddenly it begins to bend and sway in a fresh wind.*

CUT TO

PATTERSON. *Silent. As before.* STARLING *follows his glance.*

CUT TO

SINGH. *Frozen.*

CUT TO

THE FIELD. *And now the field is making odd patterns—as if something unseen were moving through.*

CUT TO

PATTERSON. *Quiet. Just the wind.*

CUT TO

THE FIELD. *Nothing visible. But the odd pattern seems to be making its way across the field.*

CUT TO

SINGH *and* STARLING. *Quiet. Just the wind.*

CUT TO

THE FIELD. *The odd pattern seems to stop. Around it, the wind makes different shapes of the grass.*

CUT TO

PATTERSON, *as the wind continues to blow. He continues to stare at the spot where the pattern stopped.*

CUT TO

SINGH. *As before. Except for one thing: suddenly, he begins to shiver, as if from cold.*

CUT TO

THE BUILDING SEQUENCE.

And what we see are a lot of cuts of a lot of activity.

Huge wooden logs are carried in and hammered to each other and driven deep into the ground—the framework for the embankments.

And SINGH *carries the heaviest loads and leads the workers—and as the structure rises, he is the one darting along the top, high in the air, pulling more logs up, helping here, helping there.*

And alongside him is his assistant, ABDULLAH, a little man with glasses and very bright eyes.

Meanwhile, STARLING is leading construction on the embankment that is on the far side of the river. And he does his best, tries to help on the top part as it rises—but alas, he is a bit on the clumsy side and balance is a problem for him. But he stays with it, does well.

And PATTERSON, in tremendous spirits, helps when needed, but mostly he is dealing with other aspects of the bridge—such as the placements of the three stone foundation pillars—

—he wades into the water, climbs the structures, takes it all in—and at the start he is still in the uniform he has worn since the start of the story—but it's clumsy for labor—

—so he changes halfway through to civilian clothes—

—which is all he wears from now on.

And the workers tire in the heat—but SINGH keeps them going, working with the power of three—

—and there are accidents and explosions, injuries and falls—and HAWTHORNE appears when needed to help with the wounded—

—it's hard, brutal work—

—but gradually, the wooden structure part is finished— two huge skeletons facing each other across the Tsavo River—and now work on the roadbed is going full blast and in the river, the three foundation pillars are taking shape—

CUT TO

TONS OF RED ROCK—being shoved into the wooden skeleton to complete the embankments. As this goes on—

CUT TO

PATTERSON and SAMUEL in the river—the foundation pillar work is going very quickly.

PATTERSON stops working, looks across the river—

—movement in the grassy area on the far side.

CUT TO

SEVERAL NANDI TRIBESMEN as they rise out of the grass, gesture to SAMUEL who gestures back. THE NANDI are a tribe of powerful little men, primitive, with teeth that have been sharpened to points.

CUT TO

PATTERSON and SAMUEL watching them.

> ### PATTERSON
> What are they looking at?

> ### SAMUEL
> You—they cannot believe you're still here.

> ### PATTERSON
> Nonsense.

> ### SAMUEL
> You don't know what Tsavo means, do you?
> *(PATTERSON doesn't)*
> It means "slaughter"...

CUT TO

THE NANDI TRIBESMEN, staring at PATTERSON, shaking their heads.

CUT TO

THE TWO EMBANKMENTS, as more and more red rock is shoved and pushed into shape.

CUT TO

THE THREE FOUNDATION PILLARS—almost finished.

CUT TO

THE ROADBED. The same.

CUT TO

THE NEAR EMBANKMENT as still more rock is forced in and

CUT TO

THE FAR EMBANKMENT done at last—

CUT TO

—and SINGH *stands on the top of the near one while across the river,* PATTERSON *pulls* STARLING *to the top of the other.*

*And they all look at each other—the embankments are both finished—*THE THREE OF THEM *are flying—*

—and what they do is this: hold their hands out toward each other, in SINGH's *gesture. It's kind of become their password.*

HOLD. *A big moment for them all!*

CUT TO

SINGH'S TENT AREA.

He sits around a fire and the man is exhausted. His dinner plate is beside him, untouched. He's too tired to eat.

CUT TO

PATTERSON'S TENT AREA.

STARLING *is there, getting ready for bed. He's wiped out, too.*

CUT TO

SINGH, *going into his tent, lying down, breathes deep.*

CUT TO

STARLING *in his tent, turning out his lamp, half asleep already.*

CUT TO

PATTERSON *in his tent, closing his eyes.*

CUT TO

SINGH, *deep asleep in his tent—*

—he shares it with a dozen others and they're all deep asleep. They lie on the floor of the tent, heads together toward the center pole, feet toward the edges of the tent.

HOLD ON SINGH. *It's very dark.* HE AND HIS MEN *just lie motionless, breathing deeply.*

KEEP HOLDING.

Now the CAMERA *moves up, high into the center of the tent, looking down at the circle of men.*

KEEP HOLDING.

They don't move, not even an inch. The steady breathing is the only sound.

YES, KEEP HOLDING.

KEEP HOLDING.

Nothing is going on down there. Nothing at all.

KEEP HOLDING.

Not a goddamn thing.

KEEP ON HOLDING. <u>KEEP ON HOLDING.</u>

*And now two things happen at the same time—*SINGH's *eyes go wide—*

—and he starts to <u>slide</u> out of the tent, as if being pulled by some giant invisible wire—

CUT TO

SINGH. CLOSE UP. <u>*Screaming.*</u>

CUT TO

THE OTHER MEN IN THE TENT, *waking, staring around and*

CUT TO

SINGH *as he slides out of the tent into the night and his screams grow even louder as we*

CUT TO

THE OTHER MEN IN THE TENT *and it's like a bomb just went off, they rise, spin, cry out, stare—*

CUT TO

THE NIGHT OUTSIDE AND SINGH'S BODY *sliding along the ground. It's pitch black, and he's going head first now, face upwards and he's going at tremendous speed and what-ever the hell it is that's making this happen is something <u>we can't make out</u>—because it's so dark and because it's on the far side of the man, and his body is in our way and*

CUT TO

UP AHEAD, some bushes and

CUT TO

SINGH, his body going faster than before and his cries are weakening—

CUT TO

THE NIGHT and his body and there is no sound at all coming from him now and there is no sound from whatever it is that is making this happen—all we see, barely, is the limp body of the big man as it skims along and—

CUT TO

UP AHEAD NOW, a low clump of bushes.

CUT TO

SINGH'S BODY, coming closer and

CUT TO

THE BUSHES and as we get in on them we can tell they are thorn bushes and now—

CUT TO

SINGH, suddenly rising magically in the night, his body flying over the bushes and gone!

CUT TO

PATTERSON and STARLING, early morning, their rifles held in front of them, racing along, suddenly stopping, staring down and

CUT TO

THE GROUND. At first we can't make out much. Then we can—a spot of red.

CUT TO

PATTERSON and STARLING, hurrying on again.

CUT TO

THORN TREES, and as they force their way through them—

CUT TO

A LARGE VULTURE, wings spread wide as it floats slowly to earth—

—HOLD—

—as it lands we can see A DOZEN OTHER VULTURES are already there, surrounding *something—*

—but we can't make it out. We are in an area of grass and shadow—

—and specks of blood.

CUT TO

PATTERSON, cries out in shock and fury, fires his rifle, races forward.

CUT TO

THE VULTURES screeching and screaming, taking off, and as we watch them soar into the morning sky—

> **HAWTHORNE'S VOICE** (over)
> What the lion must have done, once he'd killed Singh, was lick his skin off so he could drink his blood—

CUT TO

THE HOSPITAL.

HAWTHORNE is examining SINGH's body, trying to be professional, but he's clearly upset—it's awful.

> **HAWTHORNE**
> —then he feasted on him, starting with his feet—

> **STARLING**
> *(even more upset)*
> —please—you needn't be so graphic—

> **HAWTHORNE**
> You intend "sorting this out" tonight?

> **PATTERSON**
> I'll try—but this feels so different—that old lion I killed could never carry off a man Singh's size.

> **STARLING**
> *(maybe a little alarmed)*
> But you said they were always old.

PATTERSON

That's what the books say...

(Now from that—)

CUT TO

FLAMES RISING IN THE DARKENING SKY. NOW—

CUT TO

ABDULLAH in tears. Where are we?

PULL BACK TO REVEAL

This is SINGH's funeral pyre.

SINGH's body is being burned.

A LOT OF INDIANS are there. We've caught sight of some of them before—they worked with SINGH on the embankment or lived with him in his tent.

There is a terrible sense of shock.

PATTERSON stands at the rear. He is terribly moved. Now, unseen by the others, he holds his hands out in SINGH's gesture one final time.

CUT TO

THE FLAMES; they continue to rise...

CUT TO

SINGH'S TENT.

Night. The flaps that were open when SINGH was alive are now shut and tied.

CUT TO

PATTERSON, the middle of the night. He is alone, fifteen feet up in a tree near SINGH's tent. He holds his rifle, ready for anything. He cannot get comfortable.

CUT TO

THE AREA—nothing, no movement.

CUT TO

SINGH'S TENT. As before.

CUT TO

THE *AREA. No sign of movement of any kind. Dead.*

CUT TO

THE MOON. *Lower in the sky. The night is growing to a close but there is still darkness.*

CUT TO

PATTERSON. *Battling fatigue—but now, for a moment, losing—his eyes, against his will, start to close, and as they do—*

CUT TO

TWO HUGE YELLOW EYES. *That's all we see, just the eyes and they are near* PATTERSON's *tree and they are staring up at him and—*

CUT TO

PATTERSON, *startled, grabbing his rifle more tightly, staring down and—*

CUT TO

THE HUGE YELLOW EYES—*only they're gone.*

CUT TO

PATTERSON, *blowing on his hands, looking toward the sky.*

CUT TO

THE SUN, RISING, THE NIGHT DONE.

CUT TO

PATTERSON, *wrinkled and weary, frustrated and sore, walking back toward his tent area. Now he stops.*

CUT TO

ABDULLAH *and a large group of workers—only they're not working. They smoke, play cards, sit around.*

CUT TO

PATTERSON, *steaming, going up to* ABDULLAH.

PATTERSON

You were contracted to work—

ABDULLAH
(gesturing around)
—malaria epidemic; very sudden.

PATTERSON

Let me see the sick.

ABDULLAH
(not backing off)
Oh, you're a doctor now, too?

PATTERSON

There is no reason for fear.

ABDULLAH

On that I choose to remain dubious.
(beat)
Two are dead now in two nights.
(And on that news—)

CUT TO

PATTERSON. Rocked. He didn't know. Behind him now, STARLING hurries up, SAMUEL alongside.

PATTERSON
(to STARLING)
Second death? Where? —

STARLING
(gesturing)
—far end of camp—man wandering alone at night. Hawthorne's examining the body now.
(beat)
There's even less of him than of Singh.

PATTERSON
(just shakes his head)
But it's crazy—the lion shouldn't be that hungry this soon.
(getting control—he looks to SAMUEL)
Samuel?

SAMUEL

We should construct thorn fences around every tent area. Fires burning at night.

PATTERSON

Fine. Get started. And a strict curfew—*no one* allowed out at night.
(*to ABDULLAH*)
Send half your men to the bridge, the rest with these two.
(*ABDULLAH nods*)
And I'm sorry for my tone earlier. But I repeat—there is no reason for fear. I will kill the lion and I will build the bridge.

ABDULLAH

Of course you will, you are white, you can do anything . . .
(*They look at each other. They
are not friends. Now—*)

CUT TO

THE THORN BUSHES WE SAW ON OUR ARRIVAL TO TSAVO.

ENDLESS NUMBERS OF THEM. There is a machete-like sound as we

CUT TO

A BUNCH OF WORKMEN, led by SAMUEL, chopping down branches. They do it with care—these are claws—

CUT TO

—STARLING, in charge of another area, and he's not hanging back, he's taking less care than the others, hacking away with his machete, moving in between bushes and

CUT TO

ONE OF THE BUSHES, SNAPPING BACK into STARLING, and STARLING taking the blow with his arms—the claws cut his clothing—

—his arms are starting to bleed—

—he is unmindful, continues to wade into the bushes, chopping at them, cutting them down. He is a good man doing a good thing and right now, he is <u>possessed</u>.

CUT TO

PATTERSON, leaving his tent area, lost in thought, going toward the bridge. Up ahead is a grassy area.

CUT TO

THE GRASSY AREA.

For a moment, nothing. Then there is the same kind of movement we saw with SINGH. *Something is making the grass move—*

—only now there is no wind . . . HOLD.

CUT TO

PATTERSON. *Did he see it? We'll never know.*

CUT TO

STARLING, *in charge of a thorn fence that is half-way finished. His clothes are shredded. A* WORKER *has finished with a section and satisfied, moves on—*

—but STARLING *is far from finished. He grabs the thorns with his bare hands, squeezes them together.*

>   STARLING
> Not good enough—look, it's got to be tighter. *Tighter.*

CUT TO

THE AREA IN WHICH HE'S BEEN WORKING. FENCES ARE WELL ALONG TOWARD COMPLETION. IT'S LATE AFTERNOON.

PULL UP

We see more fences around more camp areas.

KEEP PULLING UP

The entire place is filled with fences now, all the individual areas protected.

The skies are starting to darken—dusk is coming fast.

Fires start up. Dozens of them.

Still darker.

Now workers come racing home to their camps, anxious for safety before darkness takes over. They zig-zag this way, that way, dodging past each other, sometimes they slam into each other, fall, get up, run on—

CUT TO

THE SUN. Falling out of the sky.

CUT TO

THE CAMP. The fires rise higher. No one moves . . . HOLD.

CUT TO

STARLING in the main tent area. He is bathing his bloody hands. SAMUEL is with him. Both are exhausted.

PATTERSON brings them each drinks. They nod thanks, drain them. They stand there together, lit by the flames of their fire. You get the sense these three will be friends forever.

> ### STARLING
> What a good week.

> ### PATTERSON
> You mean nobody died?

> ### STARLING
> *(shakes his head)*
> We all worked together. Worthy deeds were accomplished. I liked the labor.
> *(beat)*
> My mother insisted on piano lessons—broke the dear woman's heart when I turned out to be tone deaf—but she still was always at me about being careful with my hands.
> *(looks at them)*
> I like the blood, is that so strange?

> ### SAMUEL
> Oh yes, I think so.
> *(STARLING smiles, starts to speak.)*

> ### PATTERSON
> Look out, Samuel, here it comes.

> ### STARLING
> Even you two must admit that it is a glorious thing, what Man can accomplish. When there is a common splendid goal, there are no limits. Think what we will accomplish when we all have God's warmth in our hearts.

*(SAMUEL's eyes have closed; he begins to
snore. PATTERSON can't help laughing)*

CUT TO

STARLING. *As good natured as ever.*

STARLING
I am immune to your disdain.
(He looks at them now)
When I came here, I had but one small goal: to convert the entire
continent of Africa.
(shakes his head)
Now I've decided to move on to something *really* difficult: I will not
rest until both of you are safely in the fold.

SAMUEL
I've had four wives, good luck.

STARLING
The struggle is the glory . . .
(HOLD ON the three friends)

CUT TO

PATTERSON, *the next morning, working with* ABDULLAH *and some others at the
bridge.*

CUT TO

STARLING *completing work on the fence from the day before. It's high and taut and
he's done a terrific job.*

CUT TO

TSAVO STATION.

A BUNCH OF OTHER MEN *are working near a large grassy field. One of the men
starts a chant. The others pick it up. It's really pretty.*

CUT TO

PATTERSON *wading into the river—he stops as the sound of the chant comes dis-
tantly to him on the wind.*

CUT TO

THE WORKMEN CHANTING LOUDER. *It's turning into a stunner of a day—glorious blue sky broken up by pale clouds.*

CUT TO

STARLING. *Pauses briefly, listening to the sound of the men.*

CUT TO

THE MEN WORKING AND SINGING. *As before.*

CUT TO

THE GRASSY FIELD. *As before—*

—except it isn't. Because if you looked carefully, something flicked in a 180 degree arc. No telling what it was, it was gone too quickly.

CUT TO

THE MEN WORKING, SINGING ON.

CUT TO

PATTERSON *waist deep in the river, listening to the sound of the men, of the birds. The sun is higher in the sky.*

CUT TO

THE GRASSY FIELD—

—and here it comes again, only the other way this time, flicking back in another 180 degree arc—

—still hard to tell for sure what it was but maybe it was this: a tail. Now quickly—

CUT TO

PATTERSON *wading out of the river as* SAMUEL *comes into view. He holds an envelope.*

SAMUEL

For you.

PATTERSON
(taking it)

Thank you, Samuel.

> **SAMUEL**
> *(watching as PATTERSON opens it)*

Good news?

> **PATTERSON**
> *(glancing at the letter)*

I expect so—it's from my wife.

> **SAMUEL**

Do you love her?

> **PATTERSON**

I do, actually; very much.

> **SAMUEL**
> *(his wonderful smile)*

You give me hope, John.
> *(As he walks away—)*

CUT TO

STARLING, *probing at the thorn fence, searching out any last weaknesses.*

Behind him now, in the tall grass, something moves.

STARLING, *intent on his work, notices nothing.*

CUT TO

THE SINGING MEN, *getting more and more into it.*

CUT TO

PATTERSON, *by the river, opening the letter.*

There is a large tree up the riverbank. It casts a large shadow.

In the shadow now, something moves.

PATTERSON, *intent on his reading, notices nothing.*

> **HELENA** (over)

Darling one—the big excitement yesterday was when some school-
children spotted a whale—
> *(pause)*

—they were looking at me, John—

CUT TO

HELENA, *in their bedroom, moving across to the window, staring out. She now has a considerable stomach.*

> **HELENA**
> That was an attempt at humor but I don't feel very funny these days. I miss you terribly and after our son—I still have total confidence— well, after he's born I think travel might be broadening. As he kicks me at night I'm quite sure he's telling me he definitely wants to come to Africa.
> *(pause)*
> Thought you might need reminding.

CUT TO

PATTERSON *by the river. He smiles, folds the letter. Now—*

CUT TO

THE SINGING WORKMEN *at Tsavo station—and they sense how good they sound, and they really concentrate on it, on making that sound even better—*

—there must be twenty of them, working and singing—

—and <u>screaming</u>!

CUT TO

PATTERSON, *turning his head sharply and*

CUT TO

STARLING, *doing the same and*

CUT TO

THE SCREAMING WORKMEN *and they're running now, running and shrieking and that's all we see,* THE WORKMEN—

—some of them run left—

—some run right—

—and now a few of them are starting to cry.

CUT TO

A FAT COOLIE running and running, glancing back, screaming louder, running on and on and

CUT TO

—a shadow on the grass—no telling what—but it's big and it's moving and

CUT TO

THE FAT COOLIE and this next goes so fast it could be a dream—or, more accurately, a nightmare—

SHOCK CUT TO

A GIGANTIC WHITE MANED LION as it leaps onto the FAT COOLIE, brings him to earth, bites his neck half in two, kills him, just-like-that.

CUT TO

PATTERSON and SAMUEL, as they race away from the river and

CUT TO

STARLING, running from the fenced area—he holds a rifle in his hands.

CUT TO

ANOTHER PART OF THE CAMP AND A DIFFERENT BUNCH OF WORKMEN—they freeze as the screams reach them and

CUT TO

PATTERSON, on the way to his tent area and

CUT TO

DIFFERENT WORKMEN listening in fear and

CUT TO

PATTERSON, racing to his tent, grabbing his rifle and cartridges and

CUT TO

STARLING, running toward the screaming sound and

CUT TO

PATTERSON, as he charges ahead, loading his rifle on the fly and

CUT TO

SAMUEL, *carrying more ammunition, running behind* PATTERSON, *keeping up and*

CUT TO

TSAVO STATION *and nothing is visible now—the men are gone and from this angle, it looks deserted and*

CUT TO

PATTERSON, *catching* STARLING, *leading him into the* TSAVO STATION *area,* SAMUEL *just behind them.*

CUT TO

A RECTANGULAR SHED, *ahead of them. They move to it, slow—*

—then they stop—

*—a sound is heard—from around the corner—the sound continues—*PATTERSON *glances at* STARLING*—the sound could be this: the crunching of bones.*

CUT TO

PATTERSON, *checking his rifle.*

CUT TO

STARLING, *doing the same.* SAMUEL, *holding the extra ammunition, moves close to* PATTERSON. *Now—*

CUT TO

PATTERSON *as he suddenly steps away from the shed, rounding the corner and as he does—*

CUT TO

THE WHITE LION, *with the* FAT COOLIE*—the lion is crunching at his feet—*

—then the lion stares toward the shed as we

CUT TO

PATTERSON, *moving out into clearer view,* STARLING *and* SAMUEL *right with him.* THE LION *is a good distance away.*

CUT TO

THE WHITE LION, a low growl coming from him as he takes the coolie's body by the shoulder, begins backing away with it.

CUT TO

PATTERSON, dropping to his knees for the shot and

CUT TO

STARLING, doing the same and

CUT TO

THE WHITE LION, growling louder and

CUT TO

PATTERSON, taking aim and

CUT TO

SAMUEL, crying out and pointing and suddenly we're into super slow motion—

—SAMUEL has pointed back toward the roof of the shed and—

—and this <u>thing</u> is suddenly there—

—this huge dark thing and it seems to suddenly appear from the flat roof of the shed and

CUT TO

THE SUN, blocked out as this dark thing moves across it, fully stretched, it seems to go on forever and

CUT TO

PATTERSON, turning around to see and

CUT TO

STARLING, turning too, and we're coming back into regular motion now as we

CUT TO

This enormous BLACK-MANED LION diving into the three, sending them all sprawling and

CUT TO

THE WHITE MANED LION *roaring and*

CUT TO

THE BLACK MANED LION *roaring, running to the other and*

CUT TO

THE TWO LIONS IN CLOSE UP.

THE GHOST *and* THE DARKNESS, *for that is how they will be referred to—*

—and THE GHOST *has blood and bits of flesh on its mouth—*

*—*THE DARKNESS *has eyes that are crazed—*

—they are destruction bringers, these two, they can kill the old and the young and the fat and the strong—

CUT TO

PATTERSON, *lying in pain, dazed, shoulder bleeding, trying to reach for his rifle and*

CUT TO

THE GHOST *and* THE DARKNESS, *the white and the black, as they move toward the field of tall grass, <u>roaring</u> and*

CUT TO

SAMUEL, *lying in pain, his leg is bleeding and*

CUT TO

PATTERSON'S RIFLE *and*

CUT TO

PATTERSON, *as he reaches it, manages to lift it and the roaring sounds are deafening now and*

CUT TO

THE TWO GIGANTIC MALES, *backing into the tall grass—*

—they roar one final time—

CUT TO

PATTERSON, *gun ready to fire but it's futile and he knows it as we*

CUT TO

THE TALL GRASS *and they're gone, the grass is full of moving patterns from the wind—that's all we see—just the grass blowing this way, that way—*

CUT TO

PATTERSON, *staggering to his feet, staring at the grassy field.*

> **PATTERSON**
> *(dazed)*
> Jesus, two of them . . .

CUT TO

SAMUEL. *Dazed too. He points.* PATTERSON *registers, turns and*

CUT TO

STARLING, LYING DEAD, *his throat ripped open.* HOLD *briefly on the young man, then—*

CUT TO

THE STATION AREA.

A train from Mombassa is slowly pulling in. And things are fairly chaotic—there is the usual activity of what is ordinarily one of the busier parts in camp—

—but now, something new has been added: ABDULLAH *is there with several dozen coolies who work under his command. They are waiting for the train.*

PATTERSON *and* SAMUEL *are there too—and at the moment,* ABDULLAH *and* PATTERSON *are in the middle of a screamer—first one of them walking away, then coming back, then the other doing the same.*

> **PATTERSON**
> *(shouting over the noise of*
> *the approaching train.)*
> —oh, sing a different song, Abdullah—
> *(gesturing toward the men who*
> *stand by the train tracks)*
> —there's nothing wrong with your men so stop telling me there is—

ABDULLAH
(advancing on PATTERSON now)
—you do not call me a liar—you know nothing of their health—consider yourself fortunate I persuaded so many to stay—consider yourself fortunate *I* have decided to stay—

PATTERSON
(losing it)
You think you matter?
(gesturing toward the train which
is close to stopping now)
—Beaumont is on that train—*he* matters—

CUT TO

PATTERSON, *moving in on* ABDULLAH *now*—

PATTERSON
He sees this chaos, he'll replace you all.

ABDULLAH
He'll replace you, too—that's all you really care about.

PATTERSON
You think so? Fine.
(finished arguing)
It's best you get out. Go. Tell all your people to go, run home where they'll be safe under the covers and when the bridge is built and the railroad is done, they can tell their women that out of all the thousands who worked here, they were the only ones to flee—
(And he wheels around, starts
to walk away as we—)

CUT TO

ABDULLAH. *Quiet, staring after* PATTERSON.

CUT TO

SAMUEL. PATTERSON *has won. As the two of them exchange a quick glance—*

CUT TO

BEAUMONT *standing in the door of a passenger car, handsome as ever. Somehow his clothes are still pressed.*

PATTERSON moves up. In a splendid mood. SAMUEL is happy too.

> **PATTERSON**
>
> Pleasant journey?

> **BEAUMONT**
> *(stepping off the train)*
>
> How could it be? I hate Africa.

Now there is the sudden sound of men singing—PATTERSON looks around and we

CUT TO

ABDULLAH and his workmen, moving away from the train—they are singing the same song that the workmen sang just before THE GHOST and THE DARKNESS attacked—it's pretty—but it's also a little unnerving.

CUT TO

BEAUMONT. Listening a moment.

> **BEAUMONT**
>
> Lovely sound—they seem happy.

> **PATTERSON**
>
> Don't they, though?

> **BEAUMONT**
>
> So work must be going well?

CUT TO

PATTERSON. He and SAMUEL share another glance.

> **PATTERSON**
> *(delicately)*
>
> Truthfully?
> *(beat)*
> There has been the occasional odd hiccup—but then, as you so wisely told me, I'd never built in Africa.

> **BEAUMONT**
>
> But overall, you're pleased?

> **SAMUEL**
> *(moving in)*
>
> I have never experienced anything like it.

BEAUMONT; *almost longingly looks back at the train.*

> **BEAUMONT**
> I almost feel like getting right back on.
> *(glances at his watch)*

CUT TO

PATTERSON *and* SAMUEL. *They do not breathe.*

CUT TO

BEAUMONT. *He really wants to leave and for a moment it looks like he just might.*

> **BEAUMONT**
> *(a sigh)*
> I suppose it would be a dereliction of duty not to at least look around.

Now ABDULLAH *wanders happily by.*

> **PATTERSON**
> *(waving)*
> Morning, friend, glorious day.

> **ABDULLAH**
> As are they all.

CUT TO

BEAUMONT. *He takes a step inside the passenger car.*

CUT TO

PATTERSON *and* SAMUEL. *Hoping.*

CUT TO

BEAUMONT. *Reluctantly returning. He has a large box.*

> **BEAUMONT**
> I do need to see Starling.

> **PATTERSON**
> *(dully)*
> Starling?

> **BEAUMONT**
> Awhile back he ordered some bibles—

(indicating the box)
—I've brought them.
(looking around)
Is he here?

                    PATTERSON
                     (beat)
Yes he is.

                    BEAUMONT
Well, I need to speak to him.

                    SAMUEL
                     (helpfully)
Let me deliver the bibles.

CUT TO

BEAUMONT. His eyes flick from one man to the other. It's over.

                    BEAUMONT
Excellent show.
                     (voice low)
Where is Starling?

CUT TO

PATTERSON. The jig is up. He gestures—

                    PATTERSON
Here he comes now.
                     (And on that—)

CUT TO

HALF A DOZEN NATIVES CARRYING STARLING'S COFFIN. They start to put it on the train and as they do—

CUT TO

BEAUMONT. <u>Stunned</u>. And <u>furious</u>! He storms off the train and we—

CUT TO

THE BRIDGE

as BEAUMONT sees it. PATTERSON and SAMUEL are with him.

Little more work has been done than the last time we saw it. A few men are working slowly.

And now there are guards with rifles patrolling it.

CUT TO

BEAUMONT. A deadly look at them. He storms off.

CUT TO

THE HOSPITAL

as BEAUMONT sees it—PATTERSON, SAMUEL, and HAWTHORNE stand quietly.

It's much more crowded than the last time. Still under control, but barely.

BEAUMONT is icy now. He gestures sharply toward HAWTHORNE to join them.

CUT TO

OUTSIDE THE HOSPITAL.

THE FOUR MEN speak low and fast—

> BEAUMONT
> What in hell is going on?

> SAMUEL
> The Ghost and the Darkness have come.

> BEAUMONT
> *(snapping)*
> In English.

> PATTERSON
> It's what the natives are calling the lions—
> *(beat)*
> —two lions have been causing trouble—

> BEAUMONT
> —what's the surprise in that, this is Africa?

> PATTERSON
> It hasn't been that simple so far.

> BEAUMONT
> What have they done besides kill Starling?

(beat)
How many have they killed?
*(PATTERSON nods for
HAWTHORNE to answer.)*

CUT TO

HAWTHORNE. *Doing his best.*

HAWTHORNE
Well, of course, I can't supply a totally accurate answer because there
are those that are actually authenticated and there are those that we
once thought were workers killing each other or deserting from camp
so any number I give is subject to error—

BEAUMONT
(cutting through)
How many?

HAWTHORNE
Thirty, I should think.

BEAUMONT
(stunned)
Christ!
(whirling on PATTERSON)
What are you doing about it?
(Now from there—)

CUT TO

SOMETHING VERY ODD:

*we are looking at a small railroad car in a deserted area. This is not near the track
but off by itself, in an area surrounded by thorn trees.*

*Several workers are erecting a cloth tent to cover it, trying to disguise the fact that
the small railroad car is, indeed, nothing but a small railroad car.*

It is difficult work and they are perspiring heavily.

PULL BACK TO REVEAL

PATTERSON and BEAUMONT looking at it.

BEAUMONT

This is supposed to be salvation?
(staring at PATTERSON)
What kind of idiocy are we dealing with here?

PATTERSON
(keeping control)
I'm calling it my "contraption"—we're going to surround it with a boma—a fence, to you—and we're going to leave a small opening opposite that door.

CUT TO

THE RAILROAD CAR. *There is, in fact, an open front door. PATTERSON gestures for BEAUMONT to follow him inside.*

CUT TO

INSIDE THE CAR AS THEY ENTER. *It has been divided in half by thick metal bars, from floor to ceiling. The bars are close together, only a few inches between them.*

PATTERSON

In that half will be bait—human bait—I'll start things off—
(points to the open doorway)
—a sliding door will fit above that and a trip wire will run across the floor.

BEAUMONT
(The smile is back)
Genius—the beast will enter, tripping the wire, the door will slide down trapping him, you, safe behind the bars, will have him at your mercy and will shoot him.
(PATTERSON nods. BEAUMONT explodes)

BEAUMONT

Are you running a high fever, man? How could you expect something as lunatic as this to succeed? How could you even conceive of it?

PATTERSON

I didn't conceive of it for the lions—I built one in India when there was trouble with a tiger.

BEAUMONT
(incredulous)
And it *worked?*

PATTERSON
(He hates to say this)
In point of fact, it didn't.
(hurrying on)
But I'm convinced the theory is sound.

CUT TO

THE TWO OF THEM. *They move outside. The tension between them is considerable.* BEAUMONT *looks at* PATTERSON *for too long a moment.*

PATTERSON
What?

BEAUMONT
I made a mistake hiring you—you're simply not up to the job.
(Silence. Then—)

CUT TO

PATTERSON. CLOSE UP.

PATTERSON
You genuinely enjoy trying to terrify people, don't you? Well, fine—
(lashing back)
—except there isn't a higher rated engineer and we both know that. And since *time* is so important to you, how long do you think it would take to find someone else qualified and bring him here?

CUT TO

BEAUMONT. *Blazing.*

BEAUMONT
Let me explain about time—you've been here three months and already two months behind. And the Germans and the French are gearing up. And I don't care about you and I don't care about the thirty dead—I care about my knighthood and if this railroad finishes on schedule, I'll get my knighthood and *I want it.*
(glancing around as SAMUEL
appears, goes to the workers)
Professional hunters may be the answer.

PATTERSON
All they'll bring is more chaos and we've plenty of that already—and

if they come in, word will get out—and what happens to your knight-hood then?

> **BEAUMONT**

I'm going to try and locate Redbeard—I assume you've heard of him.

> **PATTERSON**

Every man who's ever fired a rifle has heard of him—by the time you find him, the lions will be dead.

> **BEAUMONT**
> *(long pause)*

Very well, the job's still yours, I'll go. But if I have to return, you're finished. And I will then do everything I can to destroy your reputation. Am I not fair?
> *(The great smile flashes)*

Told you you'd hate me.
> *(And he turns, walks off.*

CUT TO

SAMUEL. *Moving up to* PATTERSON. SAMUEL *has a bag.*

> **PATTERSON**
> *(staring after BEAUMONT)*

I do hate him.
> *(takes the bag from SAMUEL,*
> *pulls out flares)*

I want you to distribute one bag of flares to every tent area—
> *(takes out a flare)*

—tell the men to light them if there's trouble—
> *(beat)*

—make it two bags.
> *(HOLD briefly, then—)*

CUT TO

PATTERSON. ALONE. THAT NIGHT. IN HIS CONTRAPTION.

A lamp burns alongside him. Across the bars, the door of the railroad car is open. Flickering shadows. Above the doorway is a thick wooden slab the size of the door. On the ground, barely visible, the trip wire.

CUT TO

THE DOORWAY. *Outside, something is moving.*

CUT TO

PATTERSON, *rifle ready, holding his breath.*

CUT TO

THE DOORWAY. *Silence. Nothing moves now.*

CUT TO

PATTERSON. *He rubs his eyes with his hands . . .*

CUT TO

FLICKERING SHADOWS *on the wall. It's later that night.*

CUT TO

PATTERSON. *The man is bleary with fatigue. He sits in a corner of the car, writing a letter.*

> **PATTERSON VOICE** (over)
>
> "Dearest . . .
>
> . . . peace and tranquility continue to abound here—the workers report each day with a smile—except for your absence, this whole adventure is providing me nothing but pleasure . . ."

CUT TO

THE FLICKERING WALLS OF THE RAILWAY CAR. *It's later still.* PATTERSON, *finished writing, stares out at the night.*

CUT TO

A FLARE, *rising brightly toward the sky.*

CUT TO

PATTERSON, *seeing the flare. The man is miserable . . .*

CUT TO

A TREE BRANCH. MANY FLOWERS AS WELL AS THE CLAW THORNS.

> **PATTERSON VOICE** (over)
>
> Fire.

The branch is destroyed, the flowers blown away.

CUT TO

PATTERSON AND THREE INDIAN COOLIES. NOT FAR FROM HIS CONTRAPTION.

The COOLIES hold rifles. They look like brothers, which they are. They also look tough. And they are that, too. THREE STREETFIGHTERS.

> PATTERSON
> *(impressed)*

Very good indeed.

> MIDDLE COOLIE
> *(He wears glasses)*

We have hunted since childhood.

> PATTERSON

All right—you'll spend your nights inside.
> *(He indicates the railroad car.*
> *The COOLIES nod)*

You'll have plenty of ammunition. You're totally protected, you have really nothing to fear.

> MIDDLE COOLIE

That is correct.
> *(beat)*

Nothing.

PATTERSON looks at the three men. Obviously, he could not have chosen better. From them—

CUT TO

THE BRIDGE. DAY.

A lot of men working under PATTERSON. Progress is slow.

CUT TO

THE BRIDGE. NIGHT.

Some men sit on the part that's been built. Spending the night there for protection. Now, they all turn and we

CUT TO

ANOTHER FLARE going off in another part of camp.

CUT TO

PATTERSON, in a tree alone, in despair.

CUT TO

THE THREE COOLIES IN THE RAILROAD CAR.

Tough as ever. Ready for anything. But nothing is happening. Silence.

CUT TO

THE BRIDGE AGAIN AS NIGHT FALLS—MORE CROWDED THAN BEFORE.

STILL MORE MEN are moving into the river. They wade til the water is up to their necks. Then they reach out, hold hands, start to sing.

CUT TO

PATTERSON moving high into a tree. He listens to the sound. Lovely.

CUT TO

MOONLIGHT ON THE WATER. The MEN stand as before, singing softly. The river here is calm, no current to speak of. The MEN are safe—

—or rather they should be.

CUT TO

THE DARKNESS swimming swiftly, his great jaws silently encircling the neck of the last man in line, pulling him silently away and as the others start to scream—

CUT TO

PATTERSON, watching another flare rise, helplessly listening.

CUT TO

A CATTLE PEN. THE CATTLE ARE NERVOUS—

—one of them kicks wildly at the wind.

They should be nervous—

—THE GHOST walks among them, chooses which one to kill, leaps on it, brings it to earth as the dust rises.

CUT TO

ANOTHER FLARE IN THE NIGHT.

CUT TO

THE HOSPITAL. DAY. PACKED.

HAWTHORNE seems overwhelmed.

CUT TO

SOMETHING.

And for a moment we don't know what it is. There is a faint light and now we see what it is we're looking at: a wire.

HOLD ON THE WIRE.

And now a paw walks across it—

—and the <u>instant</u> that happens—

CUT TO

The THREE COOLIES, the brothers, in the contraption, two of them asleep, a flickering lamp the only illumination in the railroad car and

CUT TO

THE DOOR OF THE RAILROAD CAR slamming loudly down and

PULL BACK TO REVEAL

THE DARKNESS, standing alone in one half of the railroad car—it's incredible, just incredible but PATTERSON's idea actually worked and

KEEP PULLING BACK TO REVEAL

The entire interior of the car—the thick bars separating the two halves. In one half, the huge lion. In the other, the three armed, tough coolies.

For a moment, it could be a frozen tableau—both sides are too startled and surprised to do anything but stare—

—and then all hell just <u>explodes</u> as we

CUT TO

THE DARKNESS, *and this incredible roar comes from his throat, the kind of roar that can be heard five miles away in the night but this one in the enclosed room sounds even louder and more terrifying and*

CUT TO

THE DARKNESS, *throwing his huge body at the bars and*

CUT TO

THE BARS *and both his front claws are slashing through and*

CUT TO

The THREE TOUGH COOLIES *and they retreat against the rear wall of the car.*

CUT TO

THE DARKNESS, *rage building, throwing its body at the bars again and*

CUT TO

The COOLIES, *pressed in fear against the far wall, unable to do anything but stare and*

CUT TO

THE CLAWS, *ripping at the air and*

CUT TO

THE DARKNESS, *leaping forward, smashing into the bars and*

CUT TO

THE CEILING WHERE THE BARS *are connected and the sheer power of his leap has made them jiggle just the least bit and*

CUT TO

The COOLIES, *staring up at the ceiling and*

CUT TO

THE DARKNESS AND HERE HE COMES AGAIN, *roaring and his body hits the bars and*

CUT TO

THE CEILING—*and the bars shake—*

—*but they're not giving way.*

CUT TO

The TOUGH COOLIES, *as they begin to realize this and*

CUT TO

THE DARKNESS, *clawing for them and*

CUT TO

THE DARKNESS, *raging and roaring on his side of the bars and*

CUT TO

The FIRST COOLIE, *raising his gun and*

CUT TO

The SECOND COOLIE, *his gun raised too and*

CUT TO

The THIRD BROTHER *and he's ready and*

CUT TO

ALL THREE AS THEY FIRE—

—*and reload—*

—*and fire again, and reload, and—*

CUT TO

THE RAILROAD CAR—*and suddenly the lamp is knocked over—*

—*and a fire starts, flames grow and it's starting to look like hell in there—*

—*only it gets worse as we—*

CUT TO

THE DARKNESS at the bars—

—*and suddenly* <u>*it stands up*</u>—*it seems to fill the car, towering over everything, it's like a nightmare come to kill you—*

CUT TO

The COOLIES *staring up at the giant thing, and of course they're more terrified now than they've ever been in their lives—but these are tough men and they ignore the flames, ignore the deafening roars of the beast and*

CUT TO

THE DARKNESS, *standing there, going crazy on his side of the bars, trying to knock them down but they're holding and*

CUT TO

The TOUGH COOLIES, *reloading and*

CUT TO

THE DARKNESS, *racing around the enclosed area now and he's trapped and the flames make him seem like something unalive and his eyes have never been so bright, his roars as deafening and*

CUT TO

The THREE COOLIES, *firing again and*

CUT TO

The THREE COOLIES, *firing again and*

CUT TO

THE DARKNESS, *leaping at the bars again, and they shake, sure they shake, but they keep on holding and*

CUT TO

The COOLIES, *firing, reloading, firing, reloading and as they do, something's starting to come clear—*

—amazing as it may seem, impossible as it may be to conceive, they're <u>missing</u>.

CUT TO

THE DARKNESS, *whirling on his side, roaring and leaping and*

CUT TO

The COOLIES *and sure they fire, but they're still so goddam scared and*

CUT TO

THE DOOR THAT SLID DOWN—*it's held in place by some thick wooden bars—*

—and now the COOLIES *start to hit something—the wooden bars because they begin to splinter and*

CUT TO

THE DARKNESS, *whirling, leaping at the bars and*

CUT TO

The COOLIES *firing and then—*

CUT TO

THE DOOR *as it flops open and just like that—*

CUT TO

THE DARKNESS. *Out the door and gone.* HOLD.

CUT TO

PATTERSON JUST AFTER DAWN IN THE DAMAGED RAILROAD CAR.

PATTERSON stands where THE DARKNESS *was. The* THREE COOLIES *are where they spent the night, on the other side of the bars.*

This was the lowest point yet for PATTERSON. *Not only had his notion come so close to working, he could never fully comprehend how the coolies missed. It never seemed possible—but of course, it really happened.*

> PATTERSON
>
> Not once? —you didn't hit it once? —

> MIDDLE COOLIE
>
> —I would never make excuses—but a fire broke out—the light was bad—he kept moving—

> PATTERSON
>
> —well, of course he kept moving—but he couldn't have been more than ten feet away from the three of you—surely you must have wounded the thing—

MIDDLE COOLIE
I assure you we came close many times—

ABDULLAH is in the doorway near PATTERSON now—with several dozen men. And from ABDULLAH's face, this is clearly going to be a confrontation.

MIDDLE COOLIE
—the next time we will do better.
> *(PATTERSON makes no reaction;*
> *moves outside)*

CUT TO

ABDULLAH, simmering, moving straight to PATTERSON as soon as he's out.

ABDULLAH
The next time will be as this time—The Devil has come to Tsavo—

PATTERSON
> *(not in a mood for this)*
—that's ridiculous talk and you can't seriously believe it—

ABDULLAH
> *(moving in—tension rising as*
> *others crowd behind him)*
—now you're telling me my beliefs?—I don't think so—

CUT TO

THE BUSH just beyond—something is moving—an animal? —Impossible to say.

PATTERSON
—I wasn't and you know it and don't push it—just listen—we have a problem in Tsavo—

ABDULLAH
> *(cutting in)*
—at last you're right—we do—*you* are the problem in Tsavo—

PATTERSON
—careful, Abdullah—

PATTERSON and ABDULLAH and suddenly it's dangerous.

> **ABDULLAH**
>
> You do not tell me "careful"—you do not tell me anything—you listen while I talk—
>
> *(Now suddenly a shadow seems to cross—)*

CUT TO

ABDULLAH. CLOSE UP. *His eyes widen.*

PULL BACK TO REVEAL

AN ENORMOUS PISTOL. *Pressed hard against* ABDULLAH'S *temple.*

> **MAN'S VOICE** (over)
>
> —change in plan—you listen while *I* talk—because you have a question that needs answering.
>
> *(beat)*
>
> Will I pull the trigger?

PULL BACK FURTHER TO REVEAL

REDBEARD.

We are looking at one of those legends—ageless and powerful, with a tanned face and a thick grey beard. He has seen everything and is capable of anything.

Just now he seems more than capable of killing ABDULLAH. *Very calmly, he cocks the pistol.*

> **SAMUEL** (over)
>
> It's Redbeard, Abdullah—he'll kill you.

> **REDBEARD**
>
> *(not looking around)*
>
> No hints, Samuel.

> **ABDULLAH**
>
> *(The name has registered)*
>
> You don't know all that has happened here—the Devil has come to Tsavo.

> **REDBEARD**
>
> You're right. The Devil *has* come. Look at me. I am the Devil.

CUT TO

ABDULLAH, *staring at* REDBEARD. *Right now* REDBEARD *just could be.*

> ABDULLAH
> *(louder)*

I am a man of peace.

> REDBEARD

Am I to take it you want to live?

> ABDULLAH

Most certainly. Absolutely. Yes.

> REDBEARD

Excellent decision.
> *(Now he suddenly reaches out,*
> *shakes ABDULLAH's hand)*
Your name is Abdullah? I'm sure we'll meet again. Go and enjoy the splendid morning.

> ABDULLAH
> *(dazed—leaving)*

I think it's been a pleasure.

CUT TO

REDBEARD, and now he does another surprising thing: embraces SAMUEL.

> REDBEARD
> *(three words)*

You got old.
> *(Now he releases SAMUEL,*
> *turns to PATTERSON)*
I'm sure you're John Patterson.
> *(before PATTERSON can reply)*
Stay out of my way.
> *(And without another word, he's gone)*

CUT TO

THE HOSPITAL

as REDBEARD moves through, taking it all in. It's even worse than when last we saw it—bodies crammed everywhere and always the sound of pain and sickness.

PATTERSON stands in the doorway, watching, waiting.

> PATTERSON
> *(as REDBEARD approaches)*
> I didn't have a chance to thank you.

> REDBEARD
> *(preoccupied)*
> What did I do?

> PATTERSON
> Got me out of trouble.

> REDBEARD
> *(matter of fact)*
> Nonsense—Samuel would have done something.
> *(starts to move on)*

> PATTERSON
> We need to talk.

> REDBEARD
> Let me save time—(1) you are the engineer; (2) you are in charge;
> (3) you're sorry I'm here. Right so far?
> *(PATTERSON nods)*
> Good—because (1) I am not an engineer, (2) I don't want to be in
> charge, and (3) I'm sorrier than you are that I'm here—I hate Tsavo.
> So I will help you by killing the lions and leaving, and you will help
> me by doing what I tell you so I can leave. See any problems?

> PATTERSON
> Actually, no.

> REDBEARD
> All right—let's go into battle.
> *(suddenly taking PATTERSON's hand)*
> I'm Redbeard.
> *(as they shake)*

> PATTERSON
> Somehow I guessed.
> *(As they move outside—)*

CUT TO

THE FRONT OF THE HOSPITAL.

A BUNCH OF MEN WAIT. HAWTHORNE, SAMUEL, ABDULLAH, and perhaps a dozen other worker leaders. REDBEARD and PATTERSON move to them.

> REDBEARD

Starting now, we attack them.

> ABDULLAH

How; we don't know where they are?

> REDBEARD

We'll have to make them come to us, won't we? And since there are two of them, we're going to set two plans in motion.
> *(to HAWTHORNE)*
First: we must move the entire hospital by tomorrow night.

> HAWTHORNE
> *(appalled)*

That's a terrible idea—

> REDBEARD
> *(backtracking)*

—is it, I'm sorry, but then, of course, you're the doctor, you should know.

> HAWTHORNE

Silliest thing I ever heard of—why in the world should we go through all that?

> REDBEARD
> *(charming now)*

I suppose I could answer you. I suppose I could explain that the place is so inviting, what with the smell of blood and flesh, that they have to strike. It's even possible that I tell you I found some fresh paw marks around back which means they're already contemplating feasting here.
> *(Turning on HAWTHORNE now—*
> *his voice is building)*
But I don't want to answer you because when you question me you are really saying that I don't have the least idea what I am doing, that I am nothing but an incompetent, that I am a fool.
> *(big)*
Anyone who finds me a fool, *please say so now.*

HAWTHORNE
(The words burst out)
I have been desperate for Patterson to let me move the hospital since the day he arrived.

REDBEARD
(nice smile)
Then we agree.

(And on that—)

BEGIN THE BUILDING SEQUENCE.

It was a huge effort and they got half of it done that day—but there was always the sense of impending bloodshed.

What we see first are PATTERSON and a bunch of shots of a lot of workers—laying out the dimensions of the new boma that would surround the place. This was to be by far the biggest wall fence they had in Tsavo.

And now here comes ABDULLAH leading a crowd of men, wading into a huge patch of thorn trees, cutting the thick branches down, starting to load them for carrying—

—and it's high noon now, and PATTERSON drenched with sweat, leads the start of the actual building—taking the thorn branches, bunching them together, forcing them so there is no room between them—

—and we can just begin to get the sense of what the fence will be—except at the moment it's barely a foot high—

—and now REDBEARD appears, beckons to PATTERSON, and

CUT TO

A LONG SHOT OF A FLAT GRASSY PLAIN. AFTERNOON NOW.

PATTERSON, REDBEARD, and SAMUEL walk quickly.

CUT TO

SAMUEL turning to REDBEARD and PATTERSON.

SAMUEL
Soon.

(REDBEARD nods)

> **PATTERSON**
> *(to REDBEARD)*

I have to ask—why do you need me?

> **REDBEARD**

I don't really. But understand something—even though it may take me two or three days to sort this out—
> *(PATTERSON has to smile at the phrase)*

—when I'm gone, you'll still have to build the bridge. And I don't want the men to have lost respect for you.

> **PATTERSON**
> *(kind of surprised)*

That's very considerate.

> **REDBEARD**

I'm always considerate—my mother taught me that.

CUT TO

SAMUEL, who just breaks out laughing.

> **REDBEARD**

Why do you laugh?—you don't believe she taught me?

> **SAMUEL**

I don't believe you had a mother.
> *(And as REDBEARD laughs too—)*

CUT TO

A MASAI VILLAGE as they approach. REDBEARD walks ahead.

> **PATTERSON**

You like him, don't you?

> **SAMUEL**

Oh yes. But it takes time.

> **PATTERSON**

You've known him long?

> **SAMUEL**
> *(He has)*

Since his beard was red.

CUT TO

INSIDE THE VILLAGE. AN AGED CHIEF RUNS THINGS.

REDBEARD, PATTERSON and SAMUEL stand near him. WOMEN and CHILDREN are there. Some of the children look at REDBEARD, mime shooting, fall down dead. SAMUEL translates as necessary.

SAMUEL

How many cattle?

REDBEARD

Four should do it.

SAMUEL

They will want a lot of money.

PATTERSON
(to REDBEARD)

Have you got it?

REDBEARD

No, but you do—
(beat)
—see, you were needed after all.
(to SAMUEL)
And fifty warriors at the camp before dawn.

SAMUEL
(SAMUEL explains. The MASAI
CHIEF replies. Translating)

Why so many?

REDBEARD

Because I have two plans to kill the lions—one involving the cattle, the other the men.

CUT TO

REDBEARD and PATTERSON watching as SAMUEL tells the CHIEF.

CUT TO

THE MASAI CHIEF. He moves toward REDBEARD and PATTERSON. As he speaks, SAMUEL translates quietly. There is a sadness in the CHIEF's tone.

> **SAMUEL**
> *(translating)*
> The Ghost and the Darkness have come ... and we can do nothing ...
> but if you anger them ... they will stay in Tsavo ... and life will be-
> come more unbearable, that I know ...

CUT TO

PATTERSON, *watching as* REDBEARD *replies.*

> **REDBEARD**
> *(beat)*
> Two lions are all that have come ... they're only lions, that I know.
> *(beat)*
> And I will kill them both tomorrow.
> *(HOLD BRIEFLY, then—)*

CUT TO

SHADOWS AND FIRELIGHT. IT'S NIGHT NOW.

We're not sure for a moment where we are but we can hear metallic sounds.

Now we hear voices.

> **REDBEARD VOICE** (over)
> I'll need you by me in the morning.

> **SAMUEL VOICE** (over)
> Whatever you wish.

CUT TO

WHERE WE ARE—IT'S PATTERSON'S TENT AREA. PATTERSON, REDBEARD, HAW-
THORNE, *and* SAMUEL *sit around a fire.*

They are cleaning their guns, getting ready.

A WORD ABOUT THEIR WEAPONS. PATTERSON'S *is a good rifle and he cleans it ex-
pertly.*

REDBEARD'S *surprisingly, is the oldest. And the way his hands move as he assembles
it, he might be bathing a child.*

HAWTHORNE *is the least skilled of the three. But his rifle is clearly the finest. Bigger
than the others, with great killing power.*

There is a tremendous tension—PATTERSON, HAWTHORNE, and SAMUEL show it. REDBEARD is as before.

> **HAWTHORNE**
> *(terribly tense)*
> You're certain about tomorrow?
> *(REDBEARD is)*
> But you don't seem excited.
> *(REDBEARD isn't)*

> **PATTERSON**
> You don't enjoy killing, do you?
> *(REDBEARD doesn't)*

> **HAWTHORNE**
> Then why do it?

CUT TO

REDBEARD. CLOSE UP. He stares at the fire. Then—

> **REDBEARD**
> I have a gift.

CUT TO

THE CAMPFIRE. Silence for a moment except for the sound of the weapons being reassembled. REDBEARD'S HANDS fly. His rifle is back together. He stands, nods, goes.

CUT TO

HAWTHORNE, watching him.

> **HAWTHORNE**
> Strange man.
> *(to SAMUEL)*
> Has he always been this way?

> **SAMUEL**
> Much gentler now.

> **HAWTHORNE**
> *(shakes his head on that)*
> John?—
> *(He holds out his beautiful rifle)*

Change guns with me—mine's much more powerful. I'll be finishing the hospital tomorrow so I won't be with you—but if you'll use this . . .
>   *(beat)*
. . . then I will.

PATTERSON, touched, changes weapons.

>   **PATTERSON**
Thank you.
>   *(He turns to SAMUEL)*
Why does he need you by him?

>   **SAMUEL**
He doesn't. He needs nobody. But we have hunted many times . . .
>   *(beat)*
. . . he knows I am afraid of lions . . .

HOLD ON THE FIRELIGHT UNTIL WE SHARPLY—

CUT TO

THE BRIDGE. BEFORE DAWN.

Misty—hard to see much.

Then GHOSTS appear—

KEEP HOLDING

—they're not ghosts, they're MASAI WARRIORS emerging from the mists. They are powerful and painted and they carry noisemaking equipment—tin cans and tom toms and as more and more of them materialize—

CUT TO

A HUGE THICKET.

REDBEARD, PATTERSON, and SAMUEL wait as the WARRIORS approach.

>   **REDBEARD**
>   *(whispered)*
I spotted one of them—
>   *(gesturing toward the thicket)*
—in there.

CUT TO

THE THICKET again—alive with thorn trees. Dark, filled with long dawn shadows.

CUT TO

REDBEARD and PATTERSON and SAMUEL. A lot of tension.

REDBEARD
The best way to ensure the kill when you're using trackers is for one to shoot while the other uses the trackers to force the lion toward the shooter. Have you ever led trackers?

PATTERSON
(He hasn't)
I can try.

REDBEARD
(no good)
Samuel says you killed a lion.

PATTERSON
It was probably luck—I'd rather you did the shooting.

REDBEARD
You'd never force the lion to me—and nobody *ever* got a lion with one shot by luck.
(points—hand out straight)
Around there's a clearing—you'll know it from the anthills—get there and hide and listen to the sounds—I'll make the lion come directly to you.
(He gestures for PATTERSON to take off and as he does—)

CUT TO

THE WARRIORS as REDBEARD goes to them—

REDBEARD
(as SAMUEL translates)
—all of you—spread the width of the clearing—no gaps—go—
(claps his hands once)

CUT TO

THE WARRIORS, spreading apart.

CUT TO

THE SUN. Starting to appear more strongly on the horizon.

CUT TO

PATTERSON, running like hell.

CUT TO

THE WARRIORS, moving quickly, silently.

CUT TO

A THICK CLUSTER OF THORN TREES.

CUT TO

PATTERSON, ducking his head, blasting through.

CUT TO

THE WARRIORS, starting to cover the entire width of the thicket.

CUT TO

PATTERSON, quickstepping over rocky terrain.

CUT TO

SAMUEL staying close to REDBEARD. The fear is there.

CUT TO

REDBEARD, studying the position of the WARRIORS, who are almost ready.

CUT TO

PATTERSON, circling now, racing toward a clearing, picking up speed.

CUT TO

THE WARRIORS, spread out. They look to REDBEARD.

CUT TO

REDBEARD. Not yet.

CUT TO

PATTERSON, racing into the clearing, glances around—lots of anthills.

CUT TO

AN ANTHILL, *eight feet high. It casts a long shadow.*

CUT TO

PATTERSON. *Holding* HAWTHORNE's *marvelous rifle, he slips silently into the shadow.*

HOLD ON PATTERSON—*it's almost as if he weren't there.*

CUT SHARPLY TO

REDBEARD. CLOSE UP. *Suddenly* <u>screaming</u> *and*

CUT TO

SAMUEL, *screaming too*

CUT TO

THE WHOLE LINE OF WARRIORS, *suddenly moving forward, all of them shouting and screaming and pounding on their drums and it is* <u>loud</u>

CUT TO

PATTERSON *in the shadow. The noise is faint—but he can hear it.*

CUT TO

A DOZEN DRUMMERS, *moving forward, banging away.*

CUT TO

A DOZEN MORE DRUMMERS, *even louder.*

CUT TO

REDBEARD, *moving forward, his eyes flicking ahead—*

CUT TO

THE THICKET AHEAD. *Nothing. No movement. No lion.*

CUT TO

PATTERSON. *Just the least bit louder now.*

CUT TO

THE WHOLE LINE OF WARRIORS, *screaming and pounding and*

CUT TO

SAMUEL—*the fear worse, dogging* REDBEARD's *steps.*

CUT TO

REDBEARD. *His eyes flicking ahead.*

CUT TO

THE THICKET AHEAD. *Nothing. No movement. No lion.*

CUT TO

PATTERSON. *It's a lot louder now. He's totally still. And he's ready.*

CUT TO

THE DENSEST PART OF THE THICKET *we've seen yet.*

CUT TO

THE WARRIORS, *slashing their way through, drumming and shouting and*

CUT TO

REDBEARD, *at their head, eyes, as always, flicking.*

CUT TO

THE THICKET AHEAD. *Nothing. No movement. No lion.*

CUT TO

REDBEARD—*starting to suddenly get louder and point—*

—*because something is there—*

CUT BACK TO

THE THICKET AHEAD, *and we didn't see it before, only* REDBEARD *saw it before—*

—*but now something begins to move and*

CUT TO

REDBEARD *and the* WARRIORS *and it's all going crazy now, and they're starting to move faster and*

CUT TO

PATTERSON IN THE SHADOW.

The noise had kicked up and all the time it's coming closer and

CUT TO

REDBEARD and THE WARRIORS and the movement up ahead is more distinct and THE WARRIORS are almost in a frenzy as we

CUT TO

A FLASH OF THE GHOST IN THE THICKET—eyes bright—it starts to move away from the sound—

—and toward where PATTERSON is waiting.

CUT TO

REDBEARD. Faster, screaming louder and

CUT TO

SAMUEL and the fear starting to leave and he screams louder too and

CUT TO

PATTERSON—he fingers the weapon.

CUT TO

THE GHOST, angrily retreating faster from the sound—and now instead of going straight back it begins to veer left and

CUT TO

REDBEARD, immediately spotting the shift, gesturing to THE WARRIORS to get left and

CUT TO

THE WARRIORS, shifting over as REDBEARD directed, blocking THE GHOST's intended path and

CUT TO

THE GHOST, shifting, trying to go the other way this time and

CUT TO

REDBEARD; he spots that too, gestures for THE WARRIORS to shift the other way and

CUT TO

THE WARRIORS, *racing to their new position, blocking the animal's path again and*

CUT TO

THE GHOST, *rattled, upset, and now it starts retreating back in the original direction—toward* PATTERSON *and*

CUT TO

REDBEARD AND THE WHOLE LONG LINE OF MEN, *and it's as if mass hysteria has gripped them, because their sound keeps building and sure, their throats must ache and yes, their arms must tire, but you couldn't tell that from what they're doing—*

CUT TO

PATTERSON. *Waiting by the anthill. Waiting. Then, at last—*

CUT TO

THE GHOST, *backing into view, staring back at the sound, unaware of* PATTERSON'*s existence behind him.*

CUT TO

PATTERSON. *Noiselessly he steps away from the anthill into the sunlight. He raises* HAWTHORNE'*s gun.*

CUT TO

THE GHOST, *backing toward* PATTERSON.

CUT TO

PATTERSON, *sighting along the glistening barrel.*

CUT TO

THE GHOST, *starting to turn.*

CUT TO

PATTERSON, *ready to fire.*

CUT TO

THE GHOST IN CLOSE UP, CAUGHT IN THE CROSS HAIRS OF THE RIFLE. *And now its lips go back as it sees* PATTERSON.

CUT TO

PATTERSON, CLOSE UP, *and this is it, this is the moment and as he squeezes the trigger—*

CUT TO

PATTERSON *and* THE GHOST, *and a totally unexpected sound—a dull snap—HAWTHORNE'S rifle has* <u>misfired</u>

CUT TO

THE GHOST, *unharmed and*

CUT TO

PATTERSON *desperately working the rifle, trying to make it function and*

CUT TO

THE GHOST. *It stares at* PATTERSON.

CUT TO

PATTERSON, *and the goddamn gun won't work and he's a dead man and*

CUT TO

PATTERSON *and* THE GHOST—

—and for a moment, they might be frozen in some horrible tableau—

—THEN THE GHOST <u>ROARS</u>—

CUT TO

REDBEARD *as he hears it, breaking into a wild run—*

REDBEARD
    Shoot for chrissakes!—

CUT TO

PATTERSON *standing his ground as now* THE GHOST *takes a step toward him.*

CUT TO

REDBEARD, *firing again, reloading on the move, and up ahead is the clearing and as he reaches it—*

CUT TO

THE GHOST. *Its great head turns in the direction of* REDBEARD *and*

CUT TO

REDBEARD's *position—anthills block him from getting a clear shot at the animal— he curses, races for a better position and*

CUT TO

THE GHOST. *One final stare at* PATTERSON—

—then it makes an effortless leap into the thicket—

—and it's safe and free and gone.

CUT TO

PATTERSON. CLOSE UP. <u>*Rocked*</u>.

The low point of his life.

CUT TO

SAMUEL, *catching up to* REDBEARD.

> **SAMUEL**
> Did you ever see a lion that size?

> **REDBEARD**
> Not even close.
> > *(Now he moves to* PATTERSON*)*
> What happened?

> **PATTERSON**
> > *(a whisper)*
> ...misfire...it jammed...

> **REDBEARD**
> Has it ever done that before?

> **PATTERSON**
> ...don't know...

> **SAMUEL**
> It's Hawthorne's.

CUT TO

REDBEARD. Trying for control.

REDBEARD
You exchanged weapons?
(PATTERSON nods)
You went into battle with an untried gun?
(PATTERSON nods)

CUT TO

REDBEARD. CLOSE UP. For a moment it's impossible to tell what he's going to do. It seems that a Homeric burst of fury is about to happen.

CUT TO

PATTERSON. Drained, he expects it. It's very quiet.

CUT TO

REDBEARD, studying the younger man. And when he finally speaks, his voice is surprisingly quiet.

REDBEARD
They have an expression in prizefighting: "everyone has a plan until they're hit."
(beat)
You've just been hit . . .
(beat)
. . . the getting up is up to you . . .
(And he turns, moves off and)

CUT TO

THE NEW HOSPITAL.

Nearly finished. The fence is eight feet high and HAWTHORNE is supervising men and material that are being transferred.

CUT TO

REDBEARD, checking security in the New Hospital which is close to the center of camp. (The Old Hospital was situated on the outskirts, because they wanted to keep the workers away from the sick and the wounded.) Late afternoon, now.

PATTERSON, SAMUEL and HAWTHORNE are moving with him. As are TWO EXPE-

RIENCED ORDERLIES, both armed with powerful rifles. PATTERSON is silent here, the effects of the misfire still evident on his face.

> **REDBEARD**
> *(to the ORDERLIES)*
> Gentlemen, there's no sickness smell at all here, and little blood. When we leave, close the gate securely, don't open it til morning and keep your fires high. Any questions, ask them now.
> *(They understand—now to*
> *SAMUEL and HAWTHORNE)*
> You two will sleep beautifully in your tents.
> *(beat)*
> *And stay there.*

> **SAMUEL**
> And where will you sleep beautifully?

> **REDBEARD**
> *(smile)*
> Patterson and I will be in the old hospital—where the enticing smell of sickness still lingers—
> *(beat)*
> —and by the time we're done, I promise you, the odor of blood will be irresistible.
> *(And on that—)*

CUT TO

THE OLD HOSPITAL. STARTING TO GET DARK.

REDBEARD and PATTERSON have buckets which they empty around the inside perimeter—

—buckets of blood.

CUT TO

PATTERSON and REDBEARD. Darker. They empty still more full buckets of blood. RED-BEARD seems pleased.

CUT TO

SAMUEL and HAWTHORNE, hurrying toward their camp.

CUT TO

PATTERSON and REDBEARD, leading Masai cattle into the grounds of the Old Hospital.

CUT TO

THE ORDERLIES IN THE NEW HOSPITAL, firmly closing and locking the gate.

CUT TO

PATTERSON and REDBEARD, just outside the fence of the Old Hospital—they carry many large chunks of raw meat, drop them as they move.

CUT TO

The sun. Dying . . . dying . . .

CUT TO

PATTERSON and REDBEARD. They slip inside the deserted Old Hospital, pull the gate securely shut.

CUT TO

THE CATTLE. They stand in the center of the Old Hospital, calling to each other.

CUT TO

THE NEW HOSPITAL. Full. Clean. The men are exhausted. Most are already asleep. THE ORDERLIES sit by a fire, alert for anything.

CUT TO

THE OLD HOSPITAL. PATTERSON and REDBEARD stand across from their fire, waiting. THE COWS are quiet.

CUT TO

HAWTHORNE by his fire near his tent with SAMUEL. Nervously, they drink tea.

CUT TO

THE MOON. Higher. An hour has passed. Perhaps more.

CUT TO

REDBEARD. Walking the fence perimeter.

CUT TO

PATTERSON. THE COWS are edgy. He calms the cows.

CUT TO

OUTSIDE THE OLD HOSPITAL. *The large chunks of meat are visible in the moonlight.*

CUT TO

THE NEW HOSPITAL. *The orderlies are calm.*

CUT TO

REDBEARD, *still walking the perimeter.*

CUT TO

PATTERSON *sitting by the fire, staring at the night.* REDBEARD *moves to him, speaks in a whisper.*

> **REDBEARD**
> Think about something else.

> **PATTERSON**
> Have you ever failed?

> **REDBEARD**
> (*sad smile*)
> Only in life . . .
>   (*He walks away.* PATTERSON *watches.*)

CUT TO

THE NEW HOSPITAL. THE ORDERLIES *tend the sick. Quietly.*

CUT TO

THE NIGHT AND THE MOON. *Lovely.*

CUT TO

REDBEARD. *Stalking the perimeter. No sound. The night is deadly quiet.*

CUT TO

PATTERSON. *He stalks the perimeter now too, on the far side from* REDBEARD—*and suddenly a different and frightening sound—the ripping of flesh—*

CAMERA MOVES UP

Now we can see both PATTERSON *inside and also outside where, in shadow,* THE GHOST *and* THE DARKNESS *are devouring a hunk of meat.*

REDBEARD *moves quickly across the perimeter, gestures for* PATTERSON *to switch positions with him.*

As he reaches where PATTERSON *was, the eating sound stops.*

Silence again.

PATTERSON *reaches the far side of the fence.*

Now the eating sound comes again, and again, BOTH LIONS *are outside, directly across from* PATTERSON.

CUT TO

REDBEARD *looks across the perimeter at* PATTERSON. *Whatever's going on, it's sure as hell odd.*

CUT TO

THE CATTLE—*they are very upset suddenly—one of them kicks out violently against the night—the same gesture the cattle did just before* THE GHOST *walked through their pen and killed one—*

—now a different sound is heard: <u>scratching</u>—

CUT TO

PATTERSON *and* REDBEARD *tracking the sound—*

—the main gate is starting to be pushed in. Inside the gate the ground is covered with blood stains from where they emptied their buckets.

CUT TO

THE GATE. *More pressure against it—it could give way any moment.*

CUT TO

REDBEARD *and* PATTERSON *and from the look on* REDBEARD's *face, this is it!* PATTERSON *sees this, readies his rifle and we—*

CUT TO

THE CATTLE, *going nuts and then—*

CUT TO

THE GATE. All pressure gone.

CUT TO

PATTERSON and REDBEARD. PATTERSON is furious.

> **PATTERSON**
>
> Goddammit!

> **REDBEARD**
>
> It's all right. Stay ready.
> *(indicates the blood)*
> They know it's there.

PATTERSON takes a few steps away, stares at the moon.

CUT TO

REDBEARD; he studies PATTERSON who so clearly craves redemption.

> **REDBEARD**
> *(going to him)*
> Meant to ask you—the railroad car trap. Your idea?
> *(PATTERSON nods)*
> Excellent notion—I used the same device myself once.

> **PATTERSON**
>
> But of course yours worked.

> **REDBEARD**
>
> In point of fact it didn't—but I'm convinced the idea is sound.

He goes back to walking the perimeter. PATTERSON watches him—and for the first time since the misfire, PATTERSON's mood begins to lift.

CUT TO

THE NEW HOSPITAL

and an ORDERLY, blood pouring from his throat as he lies by the fire and

CUT TO

THE SECOND ORDERLY rounding a corner, seeing the violence; before he can scream—

CUT TO

THE GHOST and THE DARKNESS *suddenly beside him, and their giant paws slap out so fast we can't follow and*

CUT TO

THE SECOND ORDERLY, *dropping to the ground, and now we're starting to spin into madness and these next cuts go like lightning.*

CUT TO

A TENT FULL OF SICK MEN *with malaria and*

CUT TO

A PAW *flashing and*

CUT TO

THE DARKNESS, *lips pulling back and*

CUT TO

A SICK MAN, *falling from his bed, blood pouring from his slashed face and*

CUT TO

TWO MORE SICK MEN, *trying to rise and*

CUT TO

THE GHOST, *leaping on them and*

CUT TO

THE DARKNESS, *eyes narrow and brilliant and*

CUT TO

A SICK COOLIE, *and he's terrified and he tries to scream—*

—the sound barely escapes him, but even so, it's the first cry we've heard and

CUT TO

THE ENTIRE CAMP, NIGHT, WITH ALL THE FIRES BURNING— AND PATTERSON'S TENT AREA IS CLOSE BY—

—but the New Hospital is on the other end, a good distance away.

CUT TO

PATTERSON *and* REDBEARD, *rifles ready—but no sound reaches them.*

CUT TO

HAWTHORNE, *out of his tent, because he's close by and he heard it and he lights a torch, starts for the gate of the camp as* SAMUEL *does his best to stop him—*

—but HAWTHORNE *rips free and we*

CUT TO

A SECOND TENT, *as it starts to collapse and*

CUT TO

THE MEDICINE TENT, *as* THE GHOST *and* THE DARKNESS *enter and*

CUT TO

MEDICINE, *flying across the tent and*

CUT TO

GLASS, *shattering and more medicine is destroyed and*

CUT TO

A BLIZZARD OF CUTS, *of lions' claws and lions' teeth and those terrible bright blazing eyes and*

CUT TO

A TENT POLE, *being pulled out of the ground and*

CUT TO

THE GHOST *and* THE DARKNESS *and what they are doing is this:* <u>destroying</u> *the New Hospital and*

CUT TO

MORE TENTS *collapsing and*

CUT TO

THE GHOST *and* THE DARKNESS. CLOSE UP. *Eyes crazed.*

CUT TO

HAWTHORNE ALONE IN THE NIGHT, *scared shitless as he runs.*

CUT TO

SHADOWS, *moving, as* HAWTHORNE's *torch lights the surroundings and*

CUT TO

HAWTHORNE, *heart pounding, looking around and then he gasps as we*

CUT TO

THE AREA NEARBY—TWO LARGE EYES *are staring at him.*

CUT TO

HAWTHORNE, *panicked, stumbling, falling, getting up, staring around—*

CUT TO

THE AREA AROUND HIM—*the eyes are gone—*

—and now there are loud shrieks in the night coming from the New Hospital area and the <u>instant</u> *they are heard*

CUT TO

REDBEARD *and* PATTERSON, *grabbing torches, throwing the gate open and they're off as we*

CUT TO

HAWTHORNE, *running toward the New Hospital just up ahead now.*

CUT TO

PATTERSON *and* REDBEARD, *tearing through the night.*

CUT TO

THE NEW HOSPITAL. *(We see all this next through* HAWTHORNE's *eyes.) The tents are all down. The place is devastated.*

CUT TO

INSIDE THE FIRST TENT. *Filled with the dead and the dying.*

CUT TO

HAWTHORNE. Ashen. Moving on.

CUT TO

PAN ALONG THE TENT

Dead. Blood. Pain.

PAN TO THE SECOND TENT

More dead.

More dying.

It's a <u>slaughterhouse</u>.

HAWTHORNE. He's crushed. His body sags. He takes a breath, his last.

THE GHOST and THE DARKNESS are on him, <u>roaring</u>.

CUT TO

PATTERSON and REDBEARD as the roar reverberates—they glance at each other—

—then they slow

Because the New Hospital has come into view.

CUT TO

REDBEARD, CLOSE UP, staring at the disaster.

And this terrible look crosses his face. For a moment, you think he's going to fall. His body seems drained of all its power. He stands there. Just stands there. Unable to move.

CUT TO

PATTERSON. And he does move. Slowly. Carefully. Into the chaos.

He stares around—The dead and the dying are everywhere. HAWTHORNE, his face clawed almost unrecognizably, lies alone.

All that's left now is this: the sound of pain.

HOLD.

Dust rises. It covers everything. Only the sound remains.

Now different sounds take over—

—an incredible babble of human voices.

AND A RAILROAD TRAIN.

PATTERSON walks through the dust. SAMUEL, a worried look on his face, is a few steps behind.

We are at the STATION AREA and it is <u>jammed</u>. A train has pulled into the station—

—only you almost can't tell it's a train: all you can see are workers climbing up, and the inside is full so the workers clamber up onto the roofs of the cars—

—covering the cars—

—everyone is leaving—

—PATTERSON can only watch.

ABDULLAH stands on one of the cars—

—the train begins to pull out of the station.

More and more workers chase after it, get pulled on.

Now the station area is empty, the flat car roofs full.

PATTERSON still watches, eyes vacant.

ABDULLAH sees him, looks away.

The train gathers speed.

Rounds a corner . . .

. . . gone . . .

PATTERSON turns from the scene, begins to walk. SAMUEL stays close behind him, the worried look still there.

CUT TO

THE OLD HOSPITAL.

A FEW AFRICAN ORDERLIES do the best they can. PATTERSON watches only a moment, walks on. SAMUEL still behind him.

CUT TO

THE CAMP *as* PATTERSON *walks through. A ghost town now. Only Africans remain.*

CUT TO

THE CONTRAPTION *where the coolies missed* THE DARKNESS. PATTERSON *looks at it a moment, walks on.*

CUT TO

THE ANTHILL IN THE CLEARING *where* PATTERSON *misfired.* PATTERSON *looks at it a moment, walks on. And now, at last—*

CUT TO

PATTERSON'S TENT AREA. *One or two Africans.* SAMUEL *darts into his tent, emerges with something, holds it out to* PATTERSON.

IT'S A NECKLACE OF LION CLAWS.

PATTERSON *makes an almost courtly bow of thanks, puts it on—he never takes it off again. He walks on alone now until at last—*

CUT TO

THE BRIDGE.

It stops abruptly, halfway done; the foundations are in place, a lot of the scaffolding, but it's useless. Late afternoon. Desolate.

REDBEARD *sits alone, high on one of the foundations. He looks as he did the night before.*

PATTERSON *walks to the top of the near embankment. He is unshaven, wrinkled, he fingers the lion claw necklace.*

For a moment, neither says a word. Then—

> **REDBEARD**
> *(out of the blue)*
> It would have been a beautiful bridge, John. I never noticed before, occupied with other business, I suppose . . .
> *(He's rambling)*
> . . . never really pay much attention to that kind of thing but I've had

the time today, nothing else on, and this . . . it's graceful and the place-
ment couldn't be prettier . . . and . . .
                    (He goes silent now, stares off)

PATTERSON
You just got hit.
                    (REDBEARD nods)
The getting up is up to you—but they're only lions—
                    (beat)
—and I'm going after them crack of dawn . . .
                    (And on that—)

CUT TO

A LONG SHOT OF A HIGH ROCKY CLIFF—

*—we haven't seen anything like it before—it's hundreds of feet tall—gorgeous early
morning light.*

As we watch, we realize there are two dots on the side of the cliff.

As we watch a moment more, we realize the dots are moving.

CAMERA MOVES CLOSER.

THE DOTS ARE PATTERSON AND REDBEARD, *working their way along the rock face.*
PATTERSON *is much more nimble. It's dangerous, of course, but neither of them
seems to have that uppermost in mind. They travel lightly—small knapsacks and
their weapons.*

CUT TO

THE TWO OF THEM *as they make it over the cliff face. They stand, stare out.*

CUT TO

WHAT THEY SEE: *the world. They move on.*

CUT TO

A RAVINE. *They are moving along the edge. It's tricky going—if you fell you wouldn't
much like it. They are both concentrating on their movements, paying no attention
to each other as* REDBEARD *starts to speak. They don't stop moving.*

REDBEARD
In my town, when I was little, there was a brute, a bully who terror-
ized the place.

> (beat)

But he was not the problem. He had a brother who was worse than he. But the brother was not the problem.

> (beat)

One or the other of them was usually in jail. The problem came when they were both free together. The two became different from either alone.

> (beat)

Alone they were only brutes. Together they became lethal, together they killed.

PATTERSON

What happened to them?

REDBEARD
> (pause)

I got big.

> (They move on)

CUT TO

PATTERSON and REDBEARD *working their way up a steep ravine. It's hard going. They help each other.*

CUT TO

PATTERSON and REDBEARD, *moving along the edge of the ravine now. Slow. Silent.* REDBEARD *stops, points—*

CUT TO

A TANGLE IN THE BUSHES AND THORNS *with one odd thing about it: there is a clearly defined archway, as if a buffalo or rhino used it as a regular passage.*

CUT TO

THE TWO OF THEM *at the archway. They look at each other, without a word move through it.*

CUT TO

THE OTHER SIDE. *A small clearing. And at the end of the clearing: a cave.*

CUT TO

THE CAVE MOUTH. *Dark.*

CUT TO

REDBEARD *and* PATTERSON. *They each check their guns, move toward it.*

CUT TO

THE CAVE MOUTH. *Closer. Suddenly it's getting eerie.*

CUT TO

REDBEARD, *moving slowly,* PATTERSON *right with him.*

CUT TO

THE CAVE MOUTH. *They're by it—*REDBEARD *squints inside.*

CUT TO

WHAT HE SEES: *it's dark and dangerous and there is a long low tunnel you have to half-crawl through.*

Without a word, they start inside.

CUT TO

REDBEARD *and* PATTERSON, *crouched low, moving through the tunnel. Ahead there is light. They move on.*

CUT TO

THE END OF THE TUNNEL—*they can see the cave beyond.*

CUT TO

REDBEARD *and* PATTERSON. *They glance down. Nothing much there—just a copper bracelet, the kind a native might wear.*

Now they move past it and as the tunnel ends, they stand up.

CUT TO

INSIDE THE CAVE—IT'S *BIG*.

CUT TO

PATTERSON *and* REDBEARD, *moving deeper into the cave. It's scary—dark with shafts of light coming from cracks in the rock. It's dank. It all feels as at any moment, the world could end.*

CUT TO

REDBEARD. CLOSE UP. *Thunderstruck*—

REDBEARD

Dear God—

(And on those words—)

CUT TO

THE FLOOR OF THE CAVE. *More copper bracelets. And still more*—

—and now <u>bones</u>—

—<u>the floor of the place is littered with human bones</u>—

—eyeless skulls peer up at them from all around.

PULL BACK TO REVEAL

The rest of the cave. We are looking at a carpet of bones.

PATTERSON

Their den?

(REDBEARD nods.)

Have you ever seen anything like this?

REDBEARD

Nobody's seen anything like this. Lions don't have caves like this—

(beat)

—they're doing it for pleasure.

CUT TO

SEVERAL TUNNELS, *dark and ominous, leading from the cave*—

—and now there is a sound from one of the tunnels—

—something is coming close and coming fast and

CUT TO

REDBEARD *and* PATTERSON *as* REDBEARD *fires into the tunnel and the sound explodes*—

CUT TO

THE TUNNEL—

—shrieks—

CUT TO

REDBEARD and PATTERSON. *What the hell is it?*

CUT TO

THE TUNNEL—*and here they come, screeching and angry—*

—bats—

—swarms of them—hundreds of them—

CUT TO

PATTERSON and REDBEARD, *diving to the ground, lying there amidst the bangles and the bones and the skulls—*

CUT TO

THE BATS. *Circling above them. Screeching louder.*

CUT TO

PATTERSON and REDBEARD, *lying very still, eyeless skulls all around, staring.*

CUT TO

THE BATS. *For a moment, it seems as if they might attack.*

CUT TO

PATTERSON and REDBEARD. *Waiting, waiting. Then—*

CUT TO

THE BATS *back into the tunnel and*

CUT TO

PATTERSON and REDBEARD, *scrambling to their feet.*

REDBEARD
One of my chief attributes is that I'm always calm.

And then without warning, from behind them, a <u>roar</u>—

CUT TO

PATTERSON *and* REDBEARD *spin around, start back toward the entrance of the cave—*

CUT TO

THE LOW ENTRANCE TUNNEL *as they scramble half-crawling through it.*

CUT TO

OUTSIDE *as they make it, stand straight, look around—*

CUT TO

THICK BUSH *beyond—another roar and sudden movement and*

CUT TO

PATTERSON *and* REDBEARD, *entering the thick bush—but carefully, because they are vulnerable now and an attack could come from anywhere—there is the sound of water—*

—slashes of light hit their eyes, making it hard to see—and they're totally vulnerable now but it doesn't stop them—the water sound gets stronger—and as they burst clear—

CUT TO

AN AMAZING PLACE—AN AREA OF FLAT ROCK SPLIT UP AHEAD BY A WIDE FAST-RUNNING WATERFALL.

CUT TO

PATTERSON *and* REDBEARD. *They look around. Nothing is there. But the spot is wide open, exposed.*

> **PATTERSON**
> *(The words pour out)*
> Where could it have gone? How could it get across the water?
> *(looks at* REDBEARD*)*
> They're only lions, yes?

> **REDBEARD**
> *(shakes his head; he doesn't know)*
> Don't they have to be? . . .

They look around a moment more. Nothing to see—

—they turn, leave, re-enter the thick bush. And now—

CUT TO

THE DARKNESS—*who knows where it is but it's there—*

—*watching* PATTERSON.

HOLD BRIEFLY ON THE DARKNESS, *then*—

CUT TO

PATTERSON'S TENT AREA. JUST BEFORE DAWN—

—*outside the fence a dreadful sound*—<u>*the crunching of bones*</u>.

PATTERSON, REDBEARD, *and* SAMUEL *emerge from tents, listen.* PATTERSON *is on one side of the area,* REDBEARD *and* SAMUEL *on the other.*

> **SAMUEL**
> *(pointing)*
Both of them over there.

He is pointing to PATTERSON's *area.* PATTERSON *goes to* REDBEARD.

> **PATTERSON**
Ever have to use a machan?
> *(*REDBEARD *hasn't)*
I did once. In India. We will tonight.
> *(Now from that—)*

CUT TO

A CLEARING. LATER IN THE DAY.

PATTERSON *leads the few remaining men in constructing an odd looking structure: four slender poles lashed together, slanting inward, with a plank tied on top, a dozen feet up in the air.* REDBEARD *and* SAMUEL *approach.*

> **PATTERSON**
They're used to people in trees, not in a clearing.
> *(indicating the plank)*
It may be tight.

> **REDBEARD**
Not for me—I'm far too bulky and it's your idea, you go up there.
> *(to* SAMUEL*)*
Take the others to the water tower for the night.

>   PATTERSON
> I'll be bait alone?

>   REDBEARD
> Yes. And I'll be in some distant tree where I can provide no assis-
> tance whatsoever.
>   *(beat)*
> Can you control your fear?

>   PATTERSON
> I'll have to.

>   REDBEARD
> I can't control mine—I'd be lost without the shame factor driving me.

>   PATTERSON
> Was that supposed to make me feel better?
>   *(REDBEARD doesn't reply. Now—)*

CUT TO

A DONKEY BEING LED IN. LATER.

THE MEN start to tie it down, across the clearing from the machan.

PATTERSON takes a long look at the machan. He tests the support poles—they're rickety.

CUT TO

DUSK. The sun quickly beginning its quick fall.

CUT TO

THE WATER TOWER IN THE STATION AREA. SAMUEL is with the remaining men who clamber up to the platform on top.

CUT TO

THE DONKEY IN THE CLEARING. Quiet.

PULL BACK TO REVEAL

REDBEARD, holding a wooden ladder that is propped against the plank. PATTERSON climbs his slow way up. It's dangerous.

CUT TO

THE PLANK as PATTERSON makes it, clambers off the ladder, manages to sit.

CUT TO

THE VIEW. Nothing is around the machan. He is totally vulnerable.

CUT TO

REDBEARD, taking the ladder down. PATTERSON tries to get comfortable. He can't.

>   REDBEARD
>   *(glancing around)*
> It's certainly the best chance they've had to kill you.

>   PATTERSON
> You think they'll come then?
>   *(REDBEARD does)*
> Why?

>   REDBEARD
>   *(not answering)*
> Good luck.

>   PATTERSON
> *Why?*

>   REDBEARD
>   *(beat)*
> Because I think they're after you.

CUT TO

PATTERSON. This registers. Finally, he nods. REDBEARD starts to leave.

>   PATTERSON
> How many do you think they've killed?

>   REDBEARD
>   *(reluctantly)*
> The most of any lions . . . a hundred . . . ?
>   *(beat)*
> Probably more.
>   *(Now REDBEARD looks up
>   at the younger man)*
> Johnny . . . ?

They study each other in the gathering darkness. They've been through a lot together, these two. They're not what they were when they first met. An emotional moment clearly is at hand.

REDBEARD

Don't fuck up.

(And he turns, never looks back, just goes)

CUT TO

PATTERSON. *He is alone now.*

CUT TO

SHADOWS. *Growing longer.*

CUT TO

SAMUEL. *On top of the water tower. The remaining men are with him.*

CUT TO

THE DONKEY. *It peers around.*

CUT TO

PATTERSON. *His fingers move slowly along his rifle barrel—*

—there is <u>no</u> noise—but you have the sense that, at any second, the world could explode.

CUT TO

THE EDGE OF THE CLEARING, *a good distance away. A bunch of trees. Nothing unusual.*

MOVE IN CLOSER:

REDBEARD, *motionless, rifle in hand, is high in the branches.*

CUT TO

THE SUN. *About to die.*

CUT TO

PATTERSON, *trying to get comfortable. It's not possible.*

CUT TO

THE DONKEY, tethered, but able to move.

CUT TO

PATTERSON, testing the machan—not a good idea—it trembles. He stops, stares out at the setting sun, the light hitting his skin, giving it color.

CUT TO

THE SUN and here's the thing about Africa—the sun doesn't just set, it literally drops out of the sky. Suddenly it's bright and in a blink it isn't. As it drops—

CUT TO

PATTERSON. CLOSE UP. It's madness that he's up there. And he knows it. And that shows.

CUT TO

THE SKY. No moon. Just thick cloud.

CUT TO

THE DONKEY. Quiet.

CUT TO

PATTERSON. On his precarious perch. He scans constantly ahead of him past the donkey.

CUT TO

THE THICK BUSH BEYOND THE DONKEY. <u>Nothing</u> moves—

CUT TO

PATTERSON. He swallows, moistening his throat. He stares down at the donkey.

CUT TO

THE DONKEY. LATER. MIDDLE OF THE NIGHT. DARK.

<u>*And now, just the begining of a mist.*</u>

CUT TO

**THE SKY. THICKER AND THICKER CLOUDS. LATER STILL.
GETTING TOWARD MORNING.**

CUT TO

PATTERSON *sitting there twelve feet up as the silence extends, listening for something,* <u>anything</u>—

—but all there is is silence.

CUT TO

THE DONKEY. *It lies still and quiet.*

CUT TO

PATTERSON, *looking around—you get the feeling he'd like to scream.*

CUT TO

THE BUSHES AROUND HIM. *The mist is getting stronger.*

CUT TO

REDBEARD *in his tree, cursing, trying to see through the growing mist.*

CUT TO

PATTERSON, *listening, listening—*

—and then there is a sound and it's so quiet you can barely hear it but to PATTERSON *it might as well be thunder—*

—from behind the donkey there has come this: the snapping of a twig.

CUT TO

THE DONKEY, *and its eyes widen—*

HOLD ON THE DONKEY.

Because now something happens that hasn't happened before: suddenly there are no colors, only tones—

—because lions can't see colors, only tones, and that's what's happening—we are looking at the donkey from the point of view of the lion—

PULL BACK TO REVEAL

THE EYES OF THE GHOST. *Watching the donkey.*

And from now on, when we are using PATTERSON'S POINT OF VIEW, everything is clouded and thick with mist, and sounds are muted.

When we are using THE GHOST'S POINT OF VIEW, everything is totally clear—and sounds are thunderous.

CUT TO

WHAT PATTERSON SEES: just mist and vaguely, bushes.

CUT TO

WHAT THE GHOST SEES: The donkey. And CAMERA begins to move closer as THE GHOST moves, just the barest few steps closer.

CUT TO

PATTERSON. Still no sound—but beyond the donkey there seems to be some movement in the bushes.

CUT TO

WHAT THE GHOST SEES: The donkey, very, very close—

CUT TO

PATTERSON. Squinting desperately at the area beyond the donkey but the mist is so thick, he can't make certain of anything.

CUT TO

WHAT THE GHOST SEES: THE DONKEY.

HOLD.

Now there is something else visible, something behind the donkey: the four legs of the platform.

HOLD.

Now we travel up the platform —the four legs grow closer together.

HOLD AS THE GHOST AT LAST SEES PATTERSON.

CUT TO

THE EYES OF THE GHOST. NARROWING.

CUT TO

PATTERSON. *Involuntarily, a shiver.*

CUT TO

WHAT THE GHOST SEES: PATTERSON, *but the angle shifts—*

—what's happening of course is this: THE GHOST *is circling around the platform in the safety of the bushes and the mist.*

CUT TO

PATTERSON, *following the whispered sound of the bushes moving. He half turns the other way quickly, making sure that nothing is behind him.*

CUT TO

WHAT THE GHOST SEES: PATTERSON *shifting as the angle continues to change.*

CUT TO

PATTERSON *as the realization hits: the beast doesn't care about the donkey anymore,* <u>*it's stalking him*</u>.

CUT TO

REDBEARD. *In the tree. The mist obscures everything.*

CUT TO

WHAT THE GHOST SEES: PATTERSON. *Still circling, still closer.*

CUT TO

PATTERSON, *and it's scary now, this thing circling and circling, always closer, never visible and his throat is dry and you know he's just dying to blast it with his weapon or scream for it to do anything but this constantly circling movement. (In truth, the lion circled him for two hours, always coming closer, never quite seen.*

CUT TO

WHAT THE GHOST SEES: PATTERSON, *always the circling around.*

CUT TO

PATTERSON, *trying to turn on his shaky plank, trying never to let the animal's position out of his sight.*

CUT TO

WHAT THE GHOST SEES: PATTERSON. Closer...

CUT TO

PATTERSON, staring, staring at the goddamn mist, about to come apart now with the tension as it builds and builds and builds and

CUT TO

WHAT THE GHOST SEES: PATTERSON. Closer.

CUT TO

PATTERSON, gripping his weapon tightly as his head keeps on turning.

CUT TO

WHAT THE GHOST SEES: PATTERSON. <u>Closer.</u>

CUT TO

PATTERSON, suddenly yelling out loud as an <u>owl</u> lands on him—that's right a goddamn owl landed on him, thinking he was a tree, almost knocking him off the plank and

CUT TO

WHAT THE GHOST SEES: PATTERSON, starting to slip off the platform and

CUT TO

PATTERSON, fighting the owl away, but his balance is going and he's trying not to fall and

CUT TO

WHAT THE GHOST SEES: PATTERSON, beginning to topple off and

CUT TO

PATTERSON, helpless, balance going, going—

CUT TO

THE GHOST, starting to charge forward and Christ he can move and as he starts his leap—

CUT TO

REDBEARD, racing from the tree to the edge of the clearing, firing his rifle, firing again and

CUT TO

THE GHOST, as this incredible <u>roar</u> comes from him, and he spins, lands, and sure, he's been hit but he's gone, back into the bushes and the night has him and

CUT TO

SUDDEN DAWN AND PATTERSON and REDBEARD, running, stopping, staring at the ground—

CUT TO

THE GROUND. Blood.

CUT TO

PATTERSON and REDBEARD, moving quickly forward again—

CUT TO

THE GROUND. More blood and . . .

CUT TO

THE TWO OF THEM, starting to slow—

CUT TO

Strange terrain—huge anthills all over, the tallest we've seen, some of them fifteen feet high, some even higher.

CUT TO

PATTERSON and REDBEARD. They separate, take different paths through the anthills.

CUT TO

REDBEARD. Alert. One step at a time.

CUT TO

PATTERSON. The same. One step at a time.

CUT TO

THE GHOST. *Crouched high up behind one of the biggest anthills, staring down at them both.*

CUT TO

REDBEARD. *He gestures for them to stop. They do. For a moment they might be statues.*

CUT TO

THE ROCKY GROUND. *Spots of blood.* REDBEARD *kneels to examine them and as he does—*

CUT TO

THE GHOST, *launched in mid-air and*

CUT TO

PATTERSON, *whirling, falling, firing and as the sound detonates—*

CUT TO

THE GHOST, *in mid-air, body twisted and—*

—and FREEZE.

Freeze on THE GHOST *silhouetted against the morning sky.*

HOLD. *Then—*

CUT TO

SAMUEL, WALKING INTO THE SHOT—

—we're by the river and this is a repeat of the earlier moment when the three men brought the old man-eater into camp—

—only now eight men appear, carrying THE GHOST—*eight is the actual number of men that it took, and as they lower the dead animal to the ground—*

CUT TO

THE GHOST—*and now there's a sudden flash of light as we*

PULL BACK TO REVEAL

BEAUMONT, *kneeling by the dead animal. He is smiling beautifully, and there is no questioning the look of triumph on his face.*

CUT TO

A PHOTOGRAPHER; *loads of bulky equipment.* PATTERSON *and* REDBEARD *stand behind him, watching him. We're in a lovely spot by the river.* PATTERSON *and* REDBEARD *have definitely been drinking.*

> **BEAUMONT**
> I think another for posterity—this is an important moment in my life.

He strikes another pose—the PHOTOGRAPHER *goes to work.*

> **BEAUMONT**
> Understand, I had help—

> **PATTERSON**
> —not a time for modesty, Bob—

> **REDBEARD**
> —undeniably your triumph.

> **BEAUMONT**
> Oh surely there's enough credit for us all—let's not forget, you did the actual shooting. Of course, *I* hired you, *I* was the general who put the team together. And generals are the ones who tend to be remembered.

> **PHOTOGRAPHER**
> Perhaps you might put your head in its mouth, sir—could be a corker.

> **BEAUMONT**
> Clever idea, I like it.

CUT TO

THE MOUTH OF THE GHOST—*it is huge—*

*—*BEAUMONT *manages to get it open—puts his head between the enormous set of teeth—he's nervous, tries to hide it when we*

CUT TO

REDBEARD *suddenly giving a loud imitation of a lion <u>roaring</u> and*

CUT TO

BEAUMONT, *surprised and frightened—*

—he jerks his head away—

—there is the sound of laughter, PATTERSON's and REDBEARD's—

—BEAUMONT tries for his smile, can't bring it off, looks around, humiliated, and as the laughter builds—

CUT TO

THE TENT AREA. NIGHT.

PATTERSON and REDBEARD flank a fire. It's a sweet moment for them, their first, no fear in the vicinity.

It should be noted they both are drinking from bottles of champagne.

It should also be noted that the PATTERSON we see is a world away from the young man who went to meet BEAUMONT. He's unshaven, his eyes have seen terrible things, he is weary, he has known failure—he is more at ease with the world.

> PATTERSON
> *(drunk)*
> I never thought I'd say this, but I'm glad you came.

> REDBEARD
> *(drunk)*
> Understood—you realize now you could never have done it without me.

> PATTERSON
> Actually, I could have done it much more easily without you, but for whatever reason, I'm glad you came.
> *(They toast each other)*

SAMUEL, with his own bottle of champagne has wandered over, joins them.

> SAMUEL
> *(drunk)*
> Where do you go next?

> REDBEARD
> Some Russian princes want to hunt the Himalayas. You?

> SAMUEL
> Help finish the railroad.

> PATTERSON
> I want to meet my son—he must be what, two months old?

They look at the fire a moment. Then—

> SAMUEL

Three years I've worked for the railroad. Now I don't know why. It seemed a good idea once.

> PATTERSON

I feel the same about the bridge. This country certainly didn't ask for it, doesn't need it.

> REDBEARD

Too soon to tell.

They look at him.

> REDBEARD

My life was shaped because someone invented gunpowder. Our lives have crossed because two lions went mad. But what if in the future the three of us do something grand for humanity? Was that worth all the lives? Too soon to tell.

> SAMUEL
> *(drinks)*

Some mysteries should not have solutions.

> REDBEARD
> *(finishes his bottle, rises,*
> *looks at PATTERSON)*

Hold your son high.
> *(And he turns, goes to his tent)*

> PATTERSON
> *(beat—quietly)*

He has children?

> SAMUEL
> *(beat—quietly)*

Once . . .

> *(HOLD ON the two in the*
> *firelight. Then—)*

CUT TO

THE STATION MASTER AT TSAVO STATION, WORKING IN HIS

OFFICE. THE NEXT DAY.

> FEMALE VOICE (over)
> I'd like to see John Patterson, please.
> *(As he looks up—)*

CUT TO

HELENA standing there in Tsavo; she looks weary from travel, but still lovely. She holds their son in her arms. The kid is adorable.

> HELENA
> Could you tell him that his wife—
> *(catches herself, smiles)*
> —that his family has come to see him.
> *(On that—)*

CUT TO

PATTERSON AT THE BRIDGE—SAMUEL hurries to him with the news—PATTERSON takes off, running and

CUT TO

TSAVO STATION and HELENA; she holds the sleeping child, walks back and forth along the shaded front of the building, no sound at all but her heels.

CUT TO

PATTERSON, running like crazy and up ahead now is the station area.

CUT TO

HELENA—and now, in the distance, she sees him and she leaves the building, walks out into the open, smiling and waving excitely and

CUT TO

PATTERSON, excitely waving back and

CUT TO

THE DARKNESS, moving out of the grassy area behind HELENA and

CUT TO

PATTERSON, suddenly screaming "Get back—back—"

CUT TO

HELENA, *and she's too far away—his words are lost on the wind—she smiles again, waves again and*

CUT TO

PATTERSON, *screaming now, all he has,* "<u>GET BACK</u>" *and*

CUT TO

HELENA, *and she still can't make out what he's saying but just the same, she stops and*

CUT TO

THE DARKNESS, *stalking silently, closing on the mother and child.*

CUT TO

HELENA, *and the baby wakes, smiles and*

CUT TO

THE DARKNESS, *starting to run and*

CUT TO

PATTERSON *and now it shows on his face—<u>he's not going to get there, he's never going to get there</u>—*

CUT TO

HELENA, *and at last she knows something is terribly wrong and she turns—*

—but too late, too late as we

CUT TO

THE DARKNESS, *flying toward her now and*

CUT TO

PATTERSON, *in agony.*

CUT TO

THE DARKNESS, *leaping on them, taking them to ground and as* HELENA *cries out helplessly—*

CUT TO

PATTERSON, *crying out helplessly and*

PULL BACK TO REVEAL

PATTERSON IN HIS TENT,

continuing to cry out until he realizes the nightmare he just had is over—

—he staggers to his tent opening, goes outside.

CUT TO

OUTSIDE. *It's dawn.* PATTERSON, *shaken, tries to rid himself of the dream. He looks around.*

REDBEARD'S *tent is ripped—*PATTERSON *runs to it—*

CUT TO

INSIDE THE TENT. *It's empty.* PATTERSON *stares around—*

—there is blood on the tent floor and quickly—

CUT TO

THE SUN. RISING.

CUT TO

PATTERSON *running wildly, rifle in hand and*

CUT TO

SAMUEL, *carrying a weapon, hurrying to keep up and*

CUT TO

PATTERSON, *flying across rough terrain and as he and* SAMUEL *splash across a small river, he gestures for them to split and they do, widening the area of search and*

CUT TO

SAMUEL, *veering off and*

CUT TO

THORN TREES, as PATTERSON rips through them, unmindful of the damage to his clothes or his skin and

CUT TO

MORE THORNS—he plunges wildly ahead and

CUT TO

A LARGE ANTHILL—it seems to be casting an unusual shadow—PATTERSON slows, rifle ready, takes a breath, moves around it—

—nothing at all—just his imagination which has been working overtime and is only getting worse—

PATTERSON stands there a moment, unsure where to go, what to do—

—and then SAMUEL'S VOICE on the wind—calling to him—

CUT TO

PATTERSON, tracking the sound—SAMUEL's voice cries out again, louder—

—PATTERSON starts to run and run, and as he rounds a bend—

CUT TO

A FIELD OF WHITE GRASS. So lovely.

With one patch in the middle that is <u>blood red</u>.

Something is moving in the blood red area.

PATTERSON has his rifle ready—

—and then SAMUEL rises from the blood red patch.

CUT TO

SAMUEL. In shock, in despair, call it what you want—he has seen something beyond imagination.

CUT TO

PATTERSON, rushing across the field of white grass, rushing to where SAMUEL stands in the patch of blood red grass—he looks down into the grass—

—clearly, REDBEARD is there and clearly he is dead. PATTERSON and SAMUEL stare mute at one another—

—and now, from frighteningly near them, comes the triumphant roar of THE DARKNESS. *They don't even react.*

CUT TO

FLAMES RISING IN THE LATE AFTERNOON.

We should already have a sense of where we are; we've done this before.

START PULLING BACK.

SAMUEL *stands there, trying to hold it together.*

KEEP PULLING BACK.

PATTERSON *stands there too, trying to hold it together.*

KEEP PULLING BACK TO REVEAL

REDBEARD'S FUNERAL FIRE. *Flames consume the body.*

Just PATTERSON *and* SAMUEL. *No one else is there.*

The flames lick at the sky . . .

HOLD . . .

CUT TO

A LARGE BABOON. ONE LEG IS TIED TO THE END OF THE BRIDGE. GETTING DARK NOW.

PULL BACK TO REVEAL

PATTERSON *and* SAMUEL, *both armed, climbing the crane tower in use at the bridge, not far from the baboon.*

> **PATTERSON**
> You're positive lions hate baboons?
>> (SAMUEL *is*)
> Pebbles?
>> (SAMUEL *holds up a bag*)
> Let's get it over with.

CUT TO

PATTERSON *and* SAMUEL *as they reach the crane tower platform, fifteen feet from the baboon.*

They help each other into position. Almost night.

CUT TO

THE *LARGE* BABOON, *baring its enormous teeth, shrieking out into the darkness.*

CUT TO

PATTERSON *and* SAMUEL *on the platform.* SAMUEL *tosses a pebble toward the baboon and the baboon cries out again, not in pain but irritation—*

CUT TO

THE PLATFORM. PATTERSON AND SAMUEL ARE FLOODED BY MOONLIGHT. IT'S THE MIDDLE OF THE NIGHT.

They're both tired. SAMUEL *throws another pebble.* THE BABOON *cries out.*

CUT TO

PATTERSON, TENSE, ON THE PLATFORM. MIDDLE OF THE NIGHT.

He's tossing pebbles now as SAMUEL *dozes.* PATTERSON *looks wild; only nervous energy is keeping him going now.*

CUT TO

THE SKY. *The moon. Peaceful—then it turns bright yellow and frightening black clouds gather and*

CUT TO

*—*PATTERSON, *blinking, coming hard back to reality because the sky is not yellow nor were there black clouds—he's starting to hallucinate.*

CUT TO

PATTERSON AND SAMUEL ON THE PLATFORM.

SAMUEL *is awake now.* PATTERSON *stares at the river which is calm.*

CUT TO

THE RIVER, *raging and black and lethal.*

CUT TO

PATTERSON, *hallucinating again.*

CUT TO

JUST BEFORE DAWN

and THE DARKNESS *suddenly is there, creeping across the bridge toward the shrieking baboon and the* <u>instant</u> *it appears—*

CUT TO

PATTERSON. *Firing—*

CUT TO

*—*THE DARKNESS, *and it's hit and it roars and goes down and—*

CUT TO

*—*PATTERSON, *turning, reaching for* SAMUEL's *rifle, grabbing it, turning back, ready to fire again—*

CUT TO

THE DARKNESS—*gone.*

CUT TO

PATTERSON *and* SAMUEL, *blinking, looking around.*

> **PATTERSON**
> Where is it?

> **SAMUEL**
> *(pointing down)*
> Underneath.
> *(beat)*
> Somewhere.

CUT TO

WHERE HE'S POINTING. *The superstructure for the bridge—it goes several levels beneath the level where the railroad will run.*

They look at each other—not good news and we find out why when we

CUT TO

EARLY MORNING LIGHT.

PATTERSON and SAMUEL climb carefully down from their platform to the railroad level. They reach the railroad level. PATTERSON releases the baboon which races away.

CUT TO

WHERE THEY ARE. At the end of the bridge where they began construction. The bridge, two thirds finished, stretches away before them.

CUT TO

They begin to walk the incomplete bridge . . . carefully . . .

. . . as they go they look down through the crevices of their level, making sure they miss nothing.

CUT TO

SAMUEL. Terrified. Holding his rifle extremely tightly.

CUT TO

PATTERSON. Ready for anything.

CUT TO

THE BRIDGE up ahead of them. There are some holes.

CUT TO

PATTERSON and SAMUEL slowing.

CUT TO

THE HOLES. The nearest one is the largest.

CUT TO

PATTERSON. He goes on tiptoe, trying to see what's in the hole.

CUT TO

THE HOLE. It seems empty.

CUT TO

PATTERSON and SAMUEL. One step forward. Another. They hold their breaths.

CUT TO

THE HOLE. It seems empty.

CUT TO

A SHOT FROM BELOW BRIDGE LEVEL—THE DARKNESS is there.

CUT TO

PATTERSON, firing.

CUT TO

THE DARKNESS, going down through another level of scaffolding.

CUT TO

PATTERSON and SAMUEL, trying to track it.

CUT TO

THE SCAFFOLDING. Nothing is visible.

CUT TO

PATTERSON and SAMUEL—Frozen. They listen—

—nothing but their breathing.

CUT TO

PATTERSON, looking around everywhere.

CUT TO

THE HOLE. Nothing.

CUT TO

THE FIRST LEVEL of scaffolding. Nothing.

CUT TO

THE SECOND LEVEL of scaffolding. Nothing.

CUT TO

SAMUEL, looking this way, that way.

SHOCK CUT TO

*THE HOLE AS THE DARKNESS JUST FUCKING <u>FLIES</u> OUT OF IT—PATTERSON falls
back and fires and THE DARKNESS is hit and goes down but it gets up and*

CUT TO

PATTERSON, turning for SAMUEL'S RIFLE—

—only SAMUEL isn't there—

—he's taken off for the trees at the end of the bridge and

CUT TO

THE DARKNESS <u>ROARING</u> AND

CUT TO

*PATTERSON and he turns, starts running too, running across the narrow half-com-
pleted bridge and it's a bitch to do it without slipping or falling and*

CUT TO

*THE DARKNESS, wounded, sure, but the mother can still run and it takes off after
PATTERSON and*

CUT TO

SAMUEL, making it to the end of the bridge and jumping for the nearest tree and

CUT TO

PATTERSON running for his life across the bridge and

CUT TO

*THE DARKNESS, closing the gap and ordinarily PATTERSON would be a dead man
but even though THE DARKNESS hasn't got its ordinary speed, it's still faster than
PATTERSON and*

CUT TO

PATTERSON, and he's never gone this fast in his life and

CUT TO

THE TREE HE'S HEADED FOR, a different one from SAMUEL'S and it's just up ahead and

CUT TO

THE DARKNESS, closing and

CUT TO

THE TREE, and

CUT TO

THE DARKNESS, springing into the air now and

CUT TO

PATTERSON, diving for the lowest branch, grabbing hold with both hands, swinging his body up as we

CUT TO

THE DARKNESS, barely missing as PATTERSON gets his body onto the branch and now comes this insane roar and

CUT TO

SAMUEL with his rifle, as he climbs higher into his tree.

CUT TO

PATTERSON in the next tree, climbing higher, until he's fifteen feet up.

CUT TO

THE DARKNESS, on the ground, circling the trunk of PATTERSON's tree, raging with frustration.

CUT TO

PATTERSON, exhausted but it's okay now, he's safe, and as he looks across at the next tree not far away where SAMUEL is—

SAMUEL
(embarrassed)

Afraid of lions.

CUT TO

PATTERSON.

PATTERSON

It's all right, Samuel—we all get hit—

(Now he shuts up fast and)

CUT TO

THE DARKNESS, *as it does this incredible thing—<u>it starts to climb the tree</u> after* PATTERSON. *Lions are cats and when they want to climb, up they go and that's what* THE DARKNESS *is doing now, going up and*

CUT TO

PATTERSON, *and it's terrifying—he reaches for the branch above, climbing higher and*

CUT TO

THE DARKNESS, *climbing higher too and the tree is sturdy but there is a four hundred pound <u>thing</u> rocking it now and*

CUT TO

PATTERSON, *going still higher but the branches are getting thinner and the tree is shaking, and he could fall—*

CUT TO

THE DARKNESS, *climbing on, nothing can stop it—*

CUT TO

PATTERSON *and* THE DARKNESS, *together in the tree, and there's no further* PATTERSON *can go and it's harder for* THE DARKNESS *too, but slowly it moves in and*

CUT TO

PATTERSON, *calling out—*

PATTERSON

Samuel!

(And he gestures for the rifle and the instant he does—)

CUT TO

SAMUEL, *and he takes the rifle between his two hands and*

CUT TO

THE DARKNESS, *steadily moving in and*

CUT TO

SAMUEL, *tossing the rifle with great care and* PATTERSON'*s less than fifteen feet away and*

CUT TO

PATTERSON, *hands out to catch it and*

CUT TO

THE RIFLE *in mid-air and*

CUT TO

PATTERSON, *both hands ready and*

CUT TO

The rifle as it barely ticks a tree branch, spins away to the ground.

CUT TO

THE DARKNESS, *almost on* PATTERSON *now and*

CUT TO

PATTERSON, *suddenly leaping out of the tree, and yes it's a long way and sure it's going to damage him but sometimes there aren't a lot of choices in this world and*

CUT TO

SAMUEL, *staring as* PATTERSON *falls and*

CUT TO

PATTERSON, *crashing hard to earth, stunned, hurt, ribs broken, leg broken and*

CUT TO

THE DARKNESS, *and it's so big it's hard for it to get room to turn but it does and*

CUT TO

PATTERSON *crawling for the rifle, and he's in terrible pain but he reaches the weapon, grabs for it and*

CUT TO

THE DARKNESS, skittering down the tree and as it reaches the ground

CUT TO

PATTERSON, forcing himself to his feet and

CUT TO

THE DARKNESS, a dozen feet away as with a roar it starts its charge.

CUT TO

PATTERSON, aims, fires and

CUT TO

THE DARKNESS, hit again and down it goes again but up it comes again and

CUT TO

PATTERSON, firing the final shot and

CUT TO

THE DARKNESS, hit again and it has to stop, it just <u>has</u> to—

—<u>but it doesn't</u>.

It roars <u>and roars</u> and moves slowly toward PATTERSON.

CUT TO

PATTERSON; all bullets gone, no place to hide.

CUT TO

THE DARKNESS. Still moving forward.

CUT TO

PATTERSON. He takes a step backwards, falls backwards over a branch, lands hard and

CUT TO

THE DARKNESS, framed between PATTERSON's legs. Six feet away, now four, now—

CUT TO

PATTERSON, helpless on the ground.

CUT TO

THE DARKNESS, *and the eyes glow—*

—a branch is on the ground in front of it—it buries its huge teeth into the branch—

—now a long dying sigh . . . and it goes to ground.

CUT TO

PATTERSON. *Can't breathe.*

CUT TO

THE DARKNESS, *dead, its teeth still buried in the tree branch.*

CUT TO

PATTERSON. CLOSE UP. *And suddenly he just empties and tears pour down his face and he begins to cry out loud, his body wracked with sobs. He manages to get to his knees, moves next to the animal—*

CUT TO

PATTERSON *and* THE DARKNESS. *Just the sound of* PATTERSON's *tears . . .*

HOLD.

KEEP HOLDING.

CAMERA BEGINS TO RISE—

—WE ARE LOOKING AT THE BRIDGE NOW—AND IT'S FINISHED!

—hundreds of people are watching as the first train goes over it—

*—*SAMUEL *is there—lighting up the world with his smile—*

—and PATTERSON's *there, too. He stands with* HELENA, *his young son in his arms.*

Everybody smiles, everybody waves, the train goes triumphantly by.

CUT TO

PATTERSON. *He looks wonderful again, vibrant and young. Watching him, you might think he hadn't been through the nightmare as he stands there, holding the boy tightly.*

But with his other hand, he fingers his lion claw necklace . . .

HOLD ON PATTERSON.

Now slowly dissolve to an African evening. Animals stretch from one horizon to the other.

> SAMUEL VOICE (over)
> Here we still wonder about them. How did they escape for nine months? And kill 135 men? And stop the railroad?
> *(beat)*
> And were they only lions?
> *(beat)*
> If you want to decide for yourself, you must go to America. They are at the Field Museum in Chicago, and even now, after they have been dead a century, if you dare to lock eyes with them . . .
> *(beat)*
> . . . you will be afraid.

In the distance, the animals continue to move.

> SAMUEL VOICE (over)
> Sleep well.

HOLD ON THE ANIMALS. They seem to go on forever . . .

FINAL FADE OUT.

THE COLLECTED WORKS OF PADDY CHAYEFSKY

This four volume collection includes Chayefsky's finest work for the stage, screen and television. Available individually or as a boxed set.

THE STAGE PLAYS include:
GIDEON • MIDDLE OF THE NIGHT • THE LATENT HETEROSEXUAL • THE TENTH MAN • THE PASSION OF JOSEF D.
$12.95 • PAPER • ISBN 1-55783-192-0

THE TELEVISION PLAYS include:
MARTY • THE MOTHER • PRINTER'S MEASURE • HOLIDAY SONG • THE BIG DEAL • BACHELOR PARTY
$12.95 • PAPER • ISBN 1-55783-191-2

THE SCREEN PLAYS VOL I include:
NETWORK • THE AMERICANIZATION OF EMILY • THE GODDESS
$14.95 • PAPER • ISBN 1-55783-193-9

THE SCREEN PLAYS VOL II include:
MARTY • HOSPITAL • ALTERED STATES
$14.95 • PAPER • ISBN 1-55783-194-7

$59.80 The Deluxe Boxed Set • ISBN 1-55783-195-5

APPLAUSE

JFK:
The Book of the Film
By Oliver Stone and Zachary Sklar

Applause is proud to present the documented screenplay of the most talked about film of the year, complete with over 300 resaerch notes by Oliver Stone.

This thorough and complete volume also includes lengthy excerpts from the JFK debate: over 200 pages of articles by such esteemed writers and commentators as Norman Mailer, Tom Wicker, Gerald Ford and others.

"*JFK: The Book of the Film* is **AN IMPORTANT RECORD OF AN UNPRECEDENTED MOMENT IN FILM HISTORY**."—Christopher Sharrett, *Cineaste*

ISBN: 1-55783-127-0 $18.95 trade paper

WILLIAM GOLDMAN FOUR SCREENPLAYS

William Goldman, master craftsman and two-time Oscar winner continues his irreverent analysis with merciless essays written expressly for this landmark edition of his screen work. Nobody covers the psychic and political terrain behind the Hollywood lot with more cynical wisdom and practical savvy than the much celebrated author of ADVENTURES IN THE SCREEN TRADE.

William Goldman won Academy Awards for BUTCH CASSIDY AND THE SUNDANCE KID and ALL THE PRESIDENT'S MEN

Includes the screenplays:

BUTCH CASSIDY AND THE SUNDANCE KID

THE PRINCESS BRIDE

MARATHON MAN

MISERY

$18.95 • PAPER • ISBN 1-55783-265-X
$25.95 • CLOTH • ISBN 1-55783-198-X

APPLAUSE

MICHAEL CAINE

ACTING IN FILM

An Actor's Take on Movie Making

Academy Award winning actor Michael Caine, internationally acclaimed for his talented performances in movies for over 25 years, reveals secrets for success on screen. *Acting in Film* is also available on video (the BBC Master Class).

"Michael Caine knows the territory...*Acting in Film* is wonderful reading, even for those who would not dream of playing 'Lets Pretend' in front of a camera. Caine's guidance, aimed at novices still dreaming of the big break, can also give hardened critics fresh insights to what it is they're seeing up there on the screen..."
   –Charles Champlin, LOS ANGELES TIMES

BOOK/PAPER: $10.95• ISBN: 1-55783-124-6
BOOK/CLOTH: $14.95 • ISBN: 0-936839-86-4
VIDEO: $29.95 • ISBN: 1-55783-034-7

APPLAUSE